Not the Ordinary
Paper, Ink or Brush

Learn Chinese Calligraphy from
Venerable Master Hsing Yun's
One-Stroke Calligraphy

CONTENTS

I • **The Origins of Chinese Calligraphy** — 6

The Development of Chinese Calligraphy

The Evolution of Chinese Calligraphy

The Causes and Motivations Behind
Venerable Master Hsing Yun's Writing of Calligraphy

II • **Equipments Used for Chinese Calligraphy** — 12

Four Treasures of the Scholar's Studio:
Paper, Ink, Brush, Ink Stone or Slab

Venerable Master Hsing Yun on Chinese Brush and Ink

III • **Materials Used in Chinese Calligraphy** — 16

Silk

Paper

The Hanging Scroll Format

IV • **Styles of Expression in Chinese Calligraphy** — 18

An artistic expression of the everyday life and that which is fun

Colophons and Inscription

Couplets

Hanging Scroll

Square Sheet

Hand Scroll or Horizontal Scroll

Fan

Not the Ordinary Paper, Ink or Brush

Calligraphy Illustrator / Venerable Master Hsing Yun
Chief Editor / Venerable Ru Chang
Executive Editor / Venerable Ru Chuan
Editor / Chen Jun-Guang
English Translator / Cherry Lai, Mia Wong, Alice Lang, Lee Chen-Hwei
English Proofreader / Annie Yang, Michael Chang
Art Designer / Hsieh Yao-Hui
Photographer / Hsueh Yung
Publisher / Fo Guang Shan Foundation for Buddhist Culture & Education
Distributor / Fo Guang Yuan Art Gallery
Address / Fo Guang Shan, No. 153, Xingtian Road, Dashu District, Kaohsiung City, Taiwan 84049
Tel / 886-7-656-1921 Ext. 1438
Fax / 886-7-656-5196
Website / http://fgsarts.fgs.org.tw
E-mail / fgs_arts@ecp.fgs.org.tw
Edition / 2nd Printing
Published Date / July 2020
Price / NT$490

ISBN: 978-957-457-549-7
All rights reserved

V • Seals Used in Chinese Calligraphy 28

Signature Seal
Non-Signature Seal
Seals as Colophons
Seals Carved in Intaglio
Seals Carved in Relief
Originality

VI • Do-It-Yourself Seal-Making 34

VII • Utilization of Calligraphy Techniques as Means of Cultivating and Circulating Buddhism Work 36

Venerable Master Hsing Yun's Utilization of
Calligraphy Techniques as Means of
Cultivating and Circulating Buddhism Work
Prof. Fu Shen

From One Stroke Calligraphy to the Words After Recovery
— See the Power of Compassion
Ven. Ru Chang / Fo Guang Yuan Art Gallery Chief Curator

The Aesthetic Philosophy of Venerable Master Hsing Yun
Ven. Ru Chang / Fo Guang Yuan Art Gallery Chief Curator

VIII • Selections of "Venerable Master Hsing Yun's One-Stroke Calligraphy" 50

Not the Ordinary Paper, Ink or Brush,
Message from Editor

The four treasures of an ancient Chinese study room included the writing brush, ink stick, paper, and ink stone. These tools were originally intended solely for writing, but in the end, they became the instruments of an art form unique to the Chinese culture known as calligraphy. Unlike ordinary writing, calligraphy, from the process of ink grinding, ink dipping to the actual writing, embodied the power to take in one's body and mind. This capability validated its important role in Buddhism cultivation. The scripture writing career formed by the spread of early Buddhist sutras has given rise to a special affinity between Buddhism and calligraphy. Even in modern times, many temples continue to have sutra calligraphy halls. Fo Guang Shan, for example, along with various other temple branches all have sutra calligraphy halls equipped with writing brushes and inks for disciples and sanghas to copy sutras.

Venerable Master Hsing Yun of Fo Guang Shan has always attached great importance to traditional Chinese culture, and he has never stopped learning self-taught calligraphy since he was young. Although monks did not just started writing calligraphy today, the patriarchs of past dynasties from Master Huai Su to Master Hong Yi of present times, have all used calligraphy as means to propagate Buddhist teachings. Therefore, Venerable Master Hsing Yun once pointed out two major contributions of Buddhism to calligraphy: Preserving the culture of calligraphy and influencing the artistic creation of calligraphy.

Venerable Master Hsing Yun's One-Stroke Calligraphy Exhibition, organized by the Fo Guang Yuan Art Gallery, has been held around the world for more than ten years. Because of the exhibition, the traditional art of calligraphy has once again attracted the attention of Chinese and foreign viewers. From the writing form of calligraphy to the seal, interests ignited related discussions. In response to public requests, we had arranged for the re-editing and reprinting of "Not the Ordinary Paper, Ink or Brush" and changed the previous pocket book format to a larger open book format for easier storage by readers.

Venerable Master Hsing Yun propagated Buddhist teachings through calligraphy, and at the same time promoted the unique aesthetics of Chinese characters to the whole world. The integration of Buddhism with art as one was formless. It is hoped that while reading this book, readers will not only learn the introductory knowledge on calligraphy, but also attain valuable insights on the Dharma from Venerable Master's calligraphy.

 • # The Origins of Chinese Calligraphy

〖 *The Development of Chinese Calligraphy* 〗

From the time of the ancient oracle-bone writing to the modern era of the Internet, no difference can be found among the words used by the Chinese people in their everyday life of the long ago past and the present day. However, there exists a special group of characters that not only has evolved alongside the art of Chinese calligraphy, but also has developed into an integral part of Chinese painting and literature. It has, thereby, acquired an everlasting significance in the history of Chinese culture, and through the passage of time, matured into an independent discipline.

Chinese characters began to take shape during the Xia, Shang and Zhou periods (ca.2205 BCE-770 BCE), from the oracle-bone script used in divinatory rituals to the bronze inscriptions cast on bronze vessels. Every state had its own system of writing that was commonly practiced by the local people. It was during the Qin and Han Dynasties that the development of Chinese calligraphy reached a pivotal point. With the unification of China by the First Emperor, Qin Shih Huang (r. 221-210 BCE), came the end of the widely diverse bronze script when the emperor decreed that the forms of written characters be standardized throughout his empire. Under the policy of the standardization of script, the small-seal script became the standard style of writing and this marked the beginning of the development of the Chinese characters.

The Spring and Autumn Period (770-476 BCE) and the Warring States Period (475-221 BCE) saw the gradual maturation of clerical-script writing, the result of a continuous process of simplification and maturation of the small-seal script. At the height of its development, clerical script was the commonly used writing style of the Han Dynasty. However, tend to the trend of the time toward simplicity and convenience, clerical script was further transformed and abbreviated. The result was the gradual formation of the standard, running and cursive scripts. Due to the gradual evolution brought about by the change of times, Chinese calligraphy entered a new era during the periods of the Wei and Jin as well as the Northern and Southern Dynasties (265-581 CE), where different scripts were sometimes combined to form a composite style of calligraphy.

As China enjoyed a period of prosperity in trade and economy during the Sui and Tang Dynasties (581-907 CE), emperors turned their attentions to calligraphy and began to acquire all kinds of calligraphic styles from north to south and east to west. A taste for refinement and elegance in the art of calligraphy drove the technique of writing the standard script to perfection. As Chinese literature reached its apex during the Song Dynasty (960-1279), the production of engraved model-stele became quite popular due in part to a concerted effort by the court to further develop the calligraphic styles of the sages before. However, the Song literati were not content with imitated models of calligraphy in standard script. Instead of continuing the tradition of past masters, they sought to develop highly expressive forms of writing and took joy in expressing their individual temperament and character. The results were beauties of individual self-expression and artistic freedom.

A spirit of revival permeated the Yuan Dynasty (1279-1368) where the calligraphy of the Jin and Tang Dynasties were greatly emphasized. The arrival of the Ming Dynasty (1368-1644) signaled a deliberate effort to expand the influence of expressionism. A wide range of new and diverse calligraphic styles were created especially through the active use of the cursive and running scripts. It was a period of calligraphic innovations that departed radically from long-accepted norms of composition and brushwork. A group of calligraphers explored idiosyncratic styles that seemed far removed from the classical models in an effort to reveal their personal characters as well as to realize their individual freedom of artistic expression; they refused to be buried by traditions and current trends.

During the Qing Dynasty (1644-1911), ancient inscriptions and pictograms from the Xia, Shang and Zhou periods as well as the Qin and Han Dynasties were being actively excavated. This great interest in the field of archaeology prompted the development of calligraphy to make a connection between the distant past and the present. Calligraphers of the time would carefully study the strokes of the archaic scripts and experiment with new styles. Their efforts finally opened a new frontier in the writings of the seal and clerical scripts.

〖 *The Evolution of Chinese Calligraphy* 〗

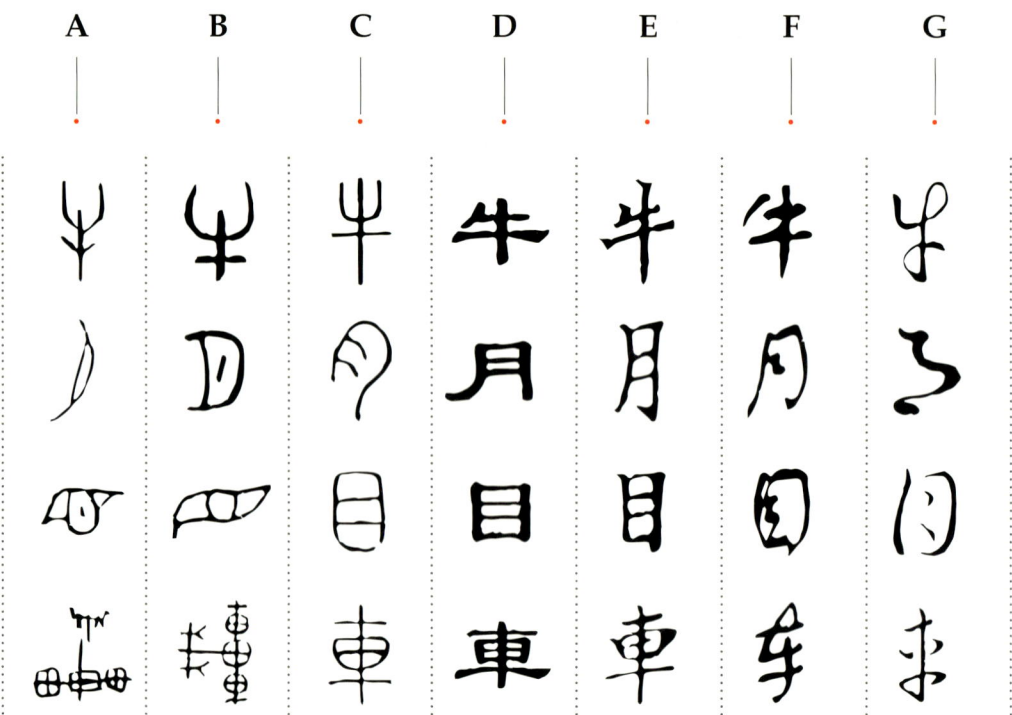

A. Oracle-Bone Writing:

Incised on animal bones and tortoise shells, oracle-bone writing, the oldest extant system of writing extant in China, served mostly as a record of divination.

B. Bronze Writing:

They were inscriptions cast on bronze vessels.

C. Small-Seal Script of the Qin Dynasty:

It was the standard style of writing after the unification of China by the First Emperor, Qin Shi Huang. The strokes are well-arranged and aesthetically beautiful, with an emphasis on regulated spacing.

D. Clerical Script:

It originated in the latter stages of the Warring States period (475- 221 BCE) and represented an important change in the history of Chinese writing.

E. Standard Script:

Widely popular during the period of the Six Dynasties (265-589), standard script began in the Western Han period (206 BCE-9 CE) as a refinement of clerical script, but without the modulated sweeping strokes or the uniform, wire-like corners of seal script.

F. Running Script:

It is between the standard and cursive scripts. It originated in the Wei kingdom (220-265 CE) and the Jin Dynasty (265-420 CE), but did not become widely popular until it reached its full maturity in the calligraphy of Wang Xizhi (307-65) and his son Wan Xianzhi (344-88).

G. Cursive Script:

It is an abbreviated form of the clerical script that was developed during the Western Han period as the demand for expediency and speed grew among the people. Although it is rapidly written with connecting strokes in lines and hooks, the abbreviated characters are still written separately and retain a trace of the clerical script. It represents the earliest form of the Chinese cursive script.

• Venerable Master Hsing Yun at the age of twenty-six.

〖 *The Causes and Motivations Behind Venerable Master Hsing Yun's Writing of Calligraphy* 〗

When Venerable Master Hsing Yun first arrived in Taiwan, he lived at Ilan's Leiyin Temple, where he discovered the causes and motivations for writing Chinese calligraphy during the annual Seven-Day Amitabha Chanting Service. Because all participants were required to abstain from speech during the service, reminders and Dharma words relating to the recitation of the Buddha's name were written in couplets and pasted on the walls of the main shrine and dining hall. These words constituted the Venerable Master's very first work of calligraphy.

"I am naturally a very shy person, who often feels ill-at-ease in front of a crowd. Since I never had any formal training in the writings of calligraphy, I would always study closely the strokes of past masters before putting down on paper what the devotees have asked me to write. Therefore, it comes as a surprise when I learned that the devotees have taken pride in collecting my handwritten calligraphy. Over the years, the writing of Dharma words as

• Venerable Master Hsing Yun and his one stroke calligraphgy

gifts has become one of my interest as I take time out from propagating the Dharma, for it is an act of sharing that will not only make the recipients happy, but myself as well. Since the days of writing calligraphy in Ilan's Leiyin Temple, I have written thousands of scrolls of calligraphy as my ways of making affinity with the devotees and showing them my gratitude. In these ways, works of granting happiness and blessing have become, for me, a work of cultivation," said the Venerable Master.

Abstinence from Speech

It is to refrain oneself from talking for the sake of containing one's karma in speech and to make introspection possible. Therefore, one must be very quiet when entering a meditation hall to practice meditation if one were to realize purity and carefreeness by means of restraining one's body and mind.

 • Equipments Used for Chinese Calligraphy

Four Treasures of the Scholar's Studio:

【 *Paper* 】

Of the four great Chinese inventions - compass, dynamite, paper and printing - two of them have to do with paper. Before the invention of paper, most of the writing was done on strips of bamboo, with each strip bearing a single column of characters and bound together to form a mat-like roll, which account for the way contemporary Chinese are read from right to left vertically. Traces of the bamboo-strip scrolls can still be found on the pages of modern-day Chinese books, where the texts are formatted in columns that are equally spaced.

【 *Ink* 】

Ink was used as black pigment for writing even before the Shang (ca.1500-1050 BCE) and Western Zhou (ca.1050-770 BCE) Dynasties. It was in Chinese calligraphy and painting that the use of ink became very important. The manufacture of ink did not reach its zenith until the Tang Dynasty (618-906). Although many different kinds of ink were produced, ink made from soot was the best suited for painting. Lampblack ink was made with lampblack from animal, vegetable or mineral oils, to which glue was mixed to give it a shiny black luster. Ink made from varnish was the blackest; and ink made from carbon obtained from burning resinous pinewood and mixed with glue was used in calligraphy. Besides having a fine texture, ink must have a very clean scent and be very fresh when applied to a piece of silk or the surface of a fan. Moreover, if one were to extend the life of an ink's glue, the ink must be stored in a cool and dry place.

【 *Brush* 】

Although the brush was used very early in Chinese history, it was not officially called the "brush" or "bi" until the unification of China by the Qin Dynasty (221-207 BCE). From the period of the Warring States (475-221 BCE) to the Qin and Han (206 BCE-220 CE) Dynasties, it was customary for government clerks to stick a brush into their hairs, so they could quickly find it for writing official documents and records. While the earliest brush was made of rabbit hair during the Tang Dynasty (618-906), goat or sheep hair was widely used after the Song Dynasty (960-1279). In its development, a variety of fibers has been employed, including the hair of the deer, fox, and wolf; the feather of the goose, duck and chicken; the bristle of the hog and rat as well as newly grown hairs, wood, bamboo and grass. When using a new brush, one must remember two things:

(1) to always loosen the fibers of the brush with cold or lukewarm water, for boiling water will do nothing but damage the pliability of the brush's tip.

(2) after each use, the brush must be rinsed off with clean water and hung upside down on a brush rack.

【 *Ink Stone or Slab* 】

Originally, ink stone was used for grinding pigments and it was not until later that it was developed into a medium on which ink was grounded. Ink stones have many different shapes: square, round or rectangular. They are made from a variety of materials: stone, ceramic, tile, brick, jade or porcelain. In the past, black ink was produced by grinding an ink cake or stick on an ink stone mixed with water. Nowadays, bottled black ink are available for pouring directly into the well or depressed area of the ink stone, without the need of rubbing an ink stick against the ink stone's surface. When using an ink stone, one must take extra care in cleaning off any dust from its surface, while making large grinding circles to prevent unnecessary indentation in the middle of the smooth, flat area. After each use, the ink stone should only be cleaned with clean cold water. It is also very important for one to be extremely careful in not getting any oil on the surface of the ink stand and never wipe it with a piece of cloth, paper or cotton. Moreover, exposure to direct sunlight is very harmful to the ink stone, so when not in use, one can fill the well with clean water and cover the whole slab with a lid to keep it moist.

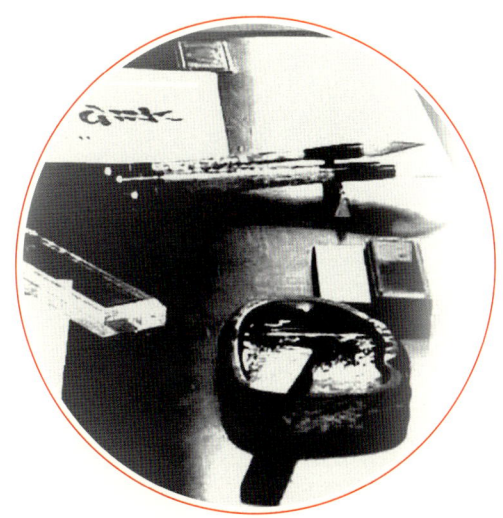

【 Venerable Master Hsing Yun on Chinese Brush and Ink 】

Since some of my devotees have learned from my diaries that I would often find time to write calligraphy for others in order to establish a good connection with them, they would bring me brushes and scrolls of fine calligraphic paper when visiting Fo Guang Shan. However, I am not very particular about what kind of brush or paper I should use, for I am not a master calligrapher by any means. Therefore, I am quite satisfied with a brush that is pliable, paper that is reasonably absorbent, and ink that is moist, smooth and of the right density.

 # Materials Used in Chinese Calligraphy

【 *Silk* 】

Traditionally, there were two kinds of materials used in Chinese calligraphy and painting–white silk and fine paper. Before the invention of paper, silk was the preferred medium of calligraphers and painters. However, the finest of silk was always sent to the imperial court to be used exclusively by the emperor and his family, thus acquiring the name "palace silk." Silk used by the common people, by contrast, was known as "yellow silk."

【 *Paper* 】

Paper was invented in China by Cai Lun during the Eastern Han Dynasty (25 CE-220CE). His student, Kong Dan, later succeeded his teacher's method of paper-making and made it his life work as he began to manufacture paper in Jing prefecture, Anhui province. According to legend, one day Kong Dan went to the mountain and came upon a downed sandalwood tree by the creek. When he saw that the tree was rotted and had thus turned white from being submerged in water for a long time, he got the idea of using it as a raw material for making paper. After a series of testing and improvements, Kong Dan was finally successful in his attempt to produce the finest paper for calligraphy and painting.

As paper became a popular medium of writing, the art of calligraphy entered a new stage of development. From the Tang Dynasty (618-906) onward, paper was mass produced and formally known as "xuanzhi," paper of the finest quality made in the Xuan district, present-day Jing prefecture.

【 *The Hanging Scroll Format* 】

(Silk and satin are used to mount a hanging scroll)

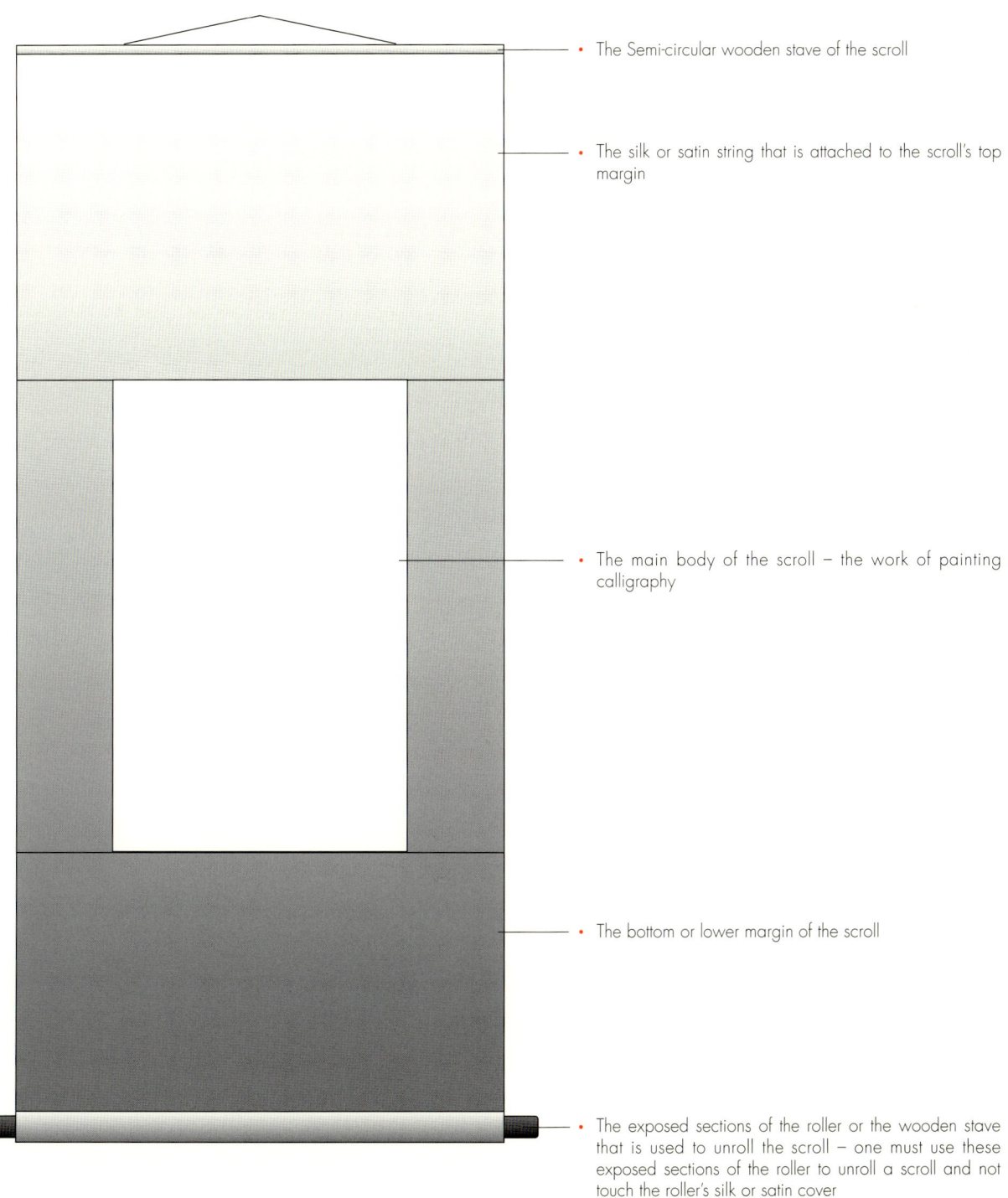

- The Semi-circular wooden stave of the scroll

- The silk or satin string that is attached to the scroll's top margin

- The main body of the scroll – the work of painting calligraphy

- The bottom or lower margin of the scroll

- The exposed sections of the roller or the wooden stave that is used to unroll the scroll – one must use these exposed sections of the roller to unroll a scroll and not touch the roller's silk or satin cover

 • **Styles of Expression in Chinese Calligraphy**

An artistic expression of the everyday life and that which is fun

From the perspective of artistic imagery, calligraphy is nothing but a drawing, because it can arose in people different feelings and emotions with its rich and impressive imageries. However, from a practical standpoint, calligraphy is nothing but words. Of all the languages in the world, only the Chinese characters can be appreciated and enjoyed as works of art, because every Chinese word is a painting in itself. Moreover, calligraphy is a traditional Chinese art form, unique to the Chinese culture. Not only is it different from the western art world in its artistic expression, but also in the materials used. The Chinese brush, for example, can bring to life the special structures of the Chinese characters on a piece of plain paper that is very absorbent, using lines that are made by inks of different density.

A work of calligraphy is not only an extraordinary achievement of the arts and letters, but also a looking glass into the world of literary study. Although calligraphy can have many different contents, they are usually composed of poems, verses, couplets, or words of inspiration authored by the calligraphers themselves, or quotes of similar types taken from famous masters. Depending on their styles of expression, these writings of calligraphy have different names.

Through artistic calligraphy works, Venerable Master Hsing Yun successfully took on the role as a cultural promoter. Every word and sentence of his writing resonates Buddha's compassionate teachings. He was able to spread Chinese calligraphy, a treasured form of art unique to the oriental culture, to every corner of this world.

【 *Colophons and Inscription* 】

Colophons or inscriptions are very important in being the fundamental parts of a painting or calligraphy, for they not only work to further substantiate and legitimatize the work in question, but also serve as contrast to bring out the main theme.

Generally speaking, colophons can be short or long in length; they are placed on the upper right-hand corner and/or the lower left-hand corner of the calligraphy or painting. When appeared on the right-hand side, a colophon usually gives the title of the work and for whom it was painted or written. Relevant poems or verses are sometimes appended. On the other hand, if a colophon is placed on the left-hand side, it usually contains the name of the calligrapher or painter as well as the date of his/her birth and the location where the work is done. If a calligraphy or painting has only a single colophon on the lower left-hand corner, it does not have a specific recipient.

• Inexhaustible Treasury
  Name of Recipient on Scroll: Nanhua University Library
  Signature of Calligrapher: 1998 Hsing Yun

【 *Couplets* 】

In traditional Chinese culture, couplets are a form of artistic expression that is not only fun and interesting, but also down-to-earth in their uses. They have always been well-liked by the people and are used for a wide variety of occasions. It is customary for the Chinese people to paste New Year couplets on their doors on New Year's Eve, which in ancient times, were known as "peach wood charm," used to ward off demons and evil spirits. Wang Anshi (1021-1086), a statesman of the Song Dynasty, once wrote a poem describing this practice of the New Year couplets: In the twilight, before the sun rises, every family will have replaced the old charm with new ones.

Originally, couplets were used in connection with the seasons, local customs, gardens, landscapes, poems and paintings. However, with the passage of time, they have developed gradually into an independent form of expression that is not only a favorite with the writers and refined scholars, but also a unique style of calligraphy.

- The bright moon sprinkled clear light from the crevices, and the clear spring water was flowing on the rocks.
Signature of Calligrapher: Hsing Yun 89

【 *Hanging Scroll* 】

Generally, a hanging scroll is of vertical format.

• Be Kind to Others
Signature of Calligrapher: Hsing Yun 88

【 *Square Sheet* 】

Square sheet is in the shape of a perfect or imperfect square.

- Selflessness
  Signature of Calligrapher: Hsing Yun

【 *Hand Scroll or Horizontal Scroll* 】

Hand scroll or horizontal scroll have different sizes, for their size is determined by the needs of the calligrapher or painter.

- Joyful and Carefree
  Date of Recipient on Scroll: 2015
  Signature of Calligrapher: Hsing Yun

【 *Fan* 】

This is an example of the round or screen fan that is generally fanned by hand. This type of fan is mostly circular in shape, with a small surface area, typically made of fine, white silk. Therefore, it is also known as "silk fan," a suitable medium of calligraphy or painting.

• Carefree
  Signature of Calligrapher: Hsing Yun

 # Seals Used in Chinese Calligraphy

On a work of calligraphy, besides the writing done by the calligrapher, there are red seals of different shapes-square, rectangle, oval or irregular–shaped–affixed to different places. There are two different kinds of seal: a signature seal and a non-signature seal. Their use is a unique feature of the art of Chinese calligraphy, for it matches the black-colored characters of the calligraphy with red impressions of the seals to produce an eye-catching work of art. By complementing the two colors of black and red, it has not only added to the overall aesthetic beauty of the work, but also served to enrich the whole composition.

【 *Signature Seal* 】

Signature seal is the calligrapher's personal name seal; it is affixed by the calligrapher to the end of his/her work when it is completely finished. Generally, a signature seal is square in shape to convey the meaning of being correct and proper. (Example: Hsing Yun)

  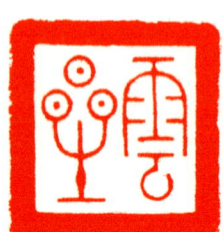

【 *Non-Signature Seal* 】

Besides name seals, all other seals are known as "non-signature seals" or "leisure seals." Despite being named as such, leisure seals have many useful functions. Having a good leisure seal is like putting the finishing touch on a work of calligraphy, for it adds to the brilliant strokes of the calligrapher. It does not only make the calligraphy more poetic in its quality, but also serve as a contrast to make its appearance more impressive. Moreover, leisure seals have a wide range of contents – they may be of poem, verses, inspirational phrases, idiom, auspicious words or images. While most of the seals appear to be rectangular or oval, some of them are of odd shapes. They are always affixed to a specially designated place. (Example: Image of Buddha and Palms Joining Bodhisattva)

【 Seals as Colophons 】

Seals had been made since the Xia, Shang and Zhou periods (2205-770 BCE) as well as the Qin and Han Dynasties (ca.221-8 BCE). Auspicious seals, a type of leisure seal, did not flourish until the Qing Dynasty (1644-1911). When a leisure seal is placed on the upper right-hand corner of the work, it functions as the "beginning seal." However, a non-signature seal is sometimes added to the end of the work at the lower left-hand corner as the "ending seal." (Example: Image of Amitabha Buddha)

【 Seals Carved in Intaglio 】

The characters are carved in intaglio against a solid background. When impressed, the characters appear to be white against a vermilion background. It is similar to a die cut with incised designs or characters. (Example: The Buddha's Light Will Forever Shine Universally)

【 Seals Carved in Relief 】

The characters are carved in relief against a background that has been removed. It is similar to a relief printing plate. (Example: The Dharma Water Will Forever Flow Incessantly)

【 Originality 】

Seals used in traditional calligraphy have their designated place of impression—at the beginning and/or at the end of the characters written—to increase the splendor of the work in general. Venerable Master Hsing Yun, in his effort to enrich the overall appearance of his calligraphy, would affix a leisure seal of "The Buddha's Light Will Forever Shine Universally; the Dharma Water Will Forever Flow Incessantly," between each column. This addition of the leisure seal by the Venerable Master functions beautifully as a contrast in making the composition more impressive.

Chinese calligraphy is not only practical, it can provide people's needs in life. It is also considered mainstream in Chinese art history with paintings. It is hung in the hall and library for people to enjoy, applied to the signboards of various institutions, shops, places of historical interest, inscriptions, etc., all of which have extremely high artistic value.

VI • Do-It-Yourself Seal-Making

In just thirty minutes, you can make a seal either for yourself or your friends and family. So, everybody, children and adults, let us get started now.

〖 *Materials* 〗

1 rock (choose a rock of any odd shape that is approximately 5-10 cm)
1 bag of paper clay or potter's clay (may be recycled for further use)
1 small paper cup
1/2 cup powdered plaster
water
clear glue
pencil
1 small pear-plate
commercial paint (red, black)
1 thin sponge

Step 1:
Making a mold for the seal: wrap 1/2 of the rock with either the paper clay or the potter's clay, see picture (1).

Step 2:
Gently remove the clay from the rock—it should be like a small water cup.

Step 3:
Pour the powdered plaster into the small papercup and fill it halfway.

Step 4:
Slowly pour the glue into the powdered plaster. Mix the powder with the glue to produce a mixture that is of the same consistency as yogurt, about 70% liquid.

Step 5:
Pour the mixture of powdered plaster and glue into the rock-shaped clay cup; fill it all the way to the top. Small air bubbles will sometimes appear on the surface of the plaster and glue mixture after it has been poured into the clay cup; slightly tap the cup on a table until the bubbles have all disappeared.

Step 6:
Cover the top of the clay cup with the small pearl-plate (the plate must be larger than the opening of the cup) to prevent spillage. Quickly turn the cup upside-down. The mixture will slowly give off heat and there is nothing to worry about.

Wait approximately 15 minutes and the mixture of powdered plaster and glue will turned to plaster. If the surface of the plaster is not smooth or is filled with small air holes, you can sand it with sandpaper.

Step 7:
After the plaster has hardened, the clay can be peeled off and the rock-shaped seal is ready for engraving.

Inverse the characters or designs when carving them on the surface of the seal, so they would appear in the right way when impressed (you can first write down the characters or draw the design on a piece of tracing paper then turn it over on top of the seal surface, so you can trace them with a pencil; but remember to press down very hard on the plaster surface in order to make a clear impression).

Step 8:
Do-It-Yourself Ink Pad: mix a little of the red paint with the black paint to produce a dark red color. Soak up the color with the thin sponge, which is then turned into an ink pad, ready for use.

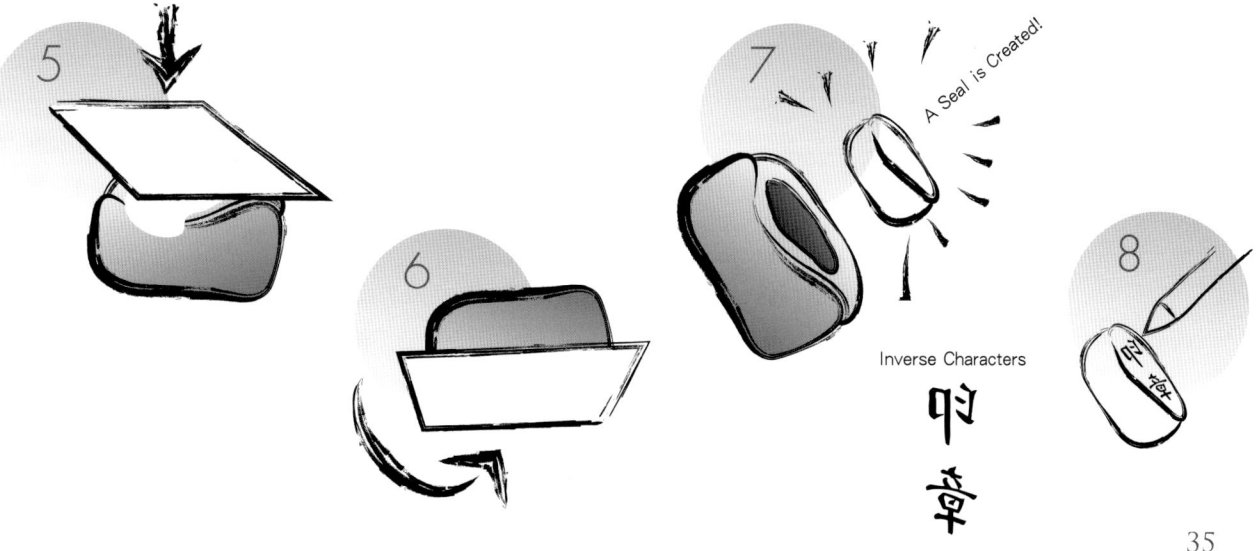

VII · Utilization of Calligraphy Techniques as Means of Cultivating and Circulating Buddhism Work

❲ *Venerable Master Hsing Yun's Utilization of Calligraphy Techniques as Means of Cultivating and Circulating Buddhism Work* ❳

Graduate Institute of Art History National Taiwan University
Prof. Fu Shen

The media of calligraphy art lies within the character of each word. Therefore, this special art must have originated from the ranks of intellectuals, and senior members of Buddhist monks must also have been the elite of such scholars. The monks of past dynasties have not only left us many Dharma words and Zen poetry, they have also left us with a lot of treasured calligraphy works given the writing brush being the only writing instrument for people in the past.

I wrote the preface for the book, "Calligraphy Exhibition of Senior Monks on Qing and Ming Dynasties." In the book chapter of "Utilizing Calligraphy as Means to Cultivate Buddhism," it made reference to the calligraphy works left behind by monks of the Sui and Tang Dynasties. While the works are hundreds or even thousands of years old, they serve as evidence of the monks' vows for Buddhism liberation and propagation at the time. With each calligraphy stroke, their determination is deeply imprinted in the depths of each viewer's heart.

Venerable Master Hsing Yun, who was born in the early twentieth century during the war, is very different from many monks in history who have exceled in calligraphy. From a young age, Venerable Master Hsing Yun was always busy learning and practicing Buddhism. He was also preoccupied with propagating the Dharma and benefiting all sentient beings. Given such, he said himself, "How can I have time to practice calligraphy?"

Therefore, Venerable Master Hsin Yun was unlike Master Hong Yi who had the opportunity to practice calligraphy before he became a monk. "During the time when I was a layperson, I have practiced calligraphy from a model for a long time." After Master Hong Yi became a monk, he still enjoyed calligraphy writing. As such he said in retrospect, "While I take deep pleasure in calligraphy, it promotes the trait of increasing heedlessness which is against Buddhist precepts." That is to say, if one writes just because one likes to write, for Buddhists, it's not worth promoting. Instead, Master Hong Yi discovered the practice of "utilizing calligraphy as means to cultivate Buddhism." "Writers can do their best to write Buddhist scriptures and spread them to the world, making all beings happy and uphold. The act of perfecting oneself for the benefit of others in acquiring enlightenment together benefits all." It can be seen that although Master Hong Yi's writing of the Buddhist scriptures was originally due to his personal interests, he has set a high attainment for his writings to achieve as much as possible. Therefore, his calligraphy not only makes all beings joyful and willing to accept and maintain faith, it also enables all beings to reach Buddhist enlightenments in the process!

I believe that in this regard, the motivation of Venerable Master Hsing Yun's writing is very different. First of all, Venerable Master is a promoter for the concepts of "Humanistic Buddhism" and "Buddhism on Life." His life was preoccupied with daily tasks and schedules, which was largely different from Master Hong Yi's monk life in the past. Venerable Master did not have time to practice writing and he feels that the words he writes are not very good. Therefore, the motivation behind Venerable Master's writing is purely simple compared to that of Master Hong Yi. His writings were not for himself at all. On the contrary, Venerable Master purely writes for the purpose of "giving joy" to his devotees. At the same time, Venerable Master also understands that the words blessed by him can also help his devotees reach enlightenment!

The ancients have said, "Calligraphy can reflect the writer's personality and emotions." That is to say, although calligraphy conveys characters, it is completely different from lifeless machine printed words. Although it is silent, "viewing a book is like viewing a person." When you see a handwriting, you can feel the writer transcending the distance of time and space and reappearing in front of you. The ancients have said, "Reading such works by a book author can help us better understand reality." The perception of such feeling is strong and does not only apply in ancient times when there was no portrait photography. Even today, when you receive a handwritten letter from a relative or friend from a distant place, it feels much more cordial than an electronic letter, as if you were actually seeing them in person.

It is for this reason, the devotees of Venerable Master Hsing Yun were eager to have his original handwritten calligraphy. Through his writings, Venerable Master's solemn and compassionate appearance and spirits immediately emerges in front of them. The Venerable Master in every piece of his work carefully selects the content of each sentence and writes them meticulously, granting one more wish with each work. Therefore, a viewer can feel the cultivation of Venerable Master's life, blessings, and teachings to all living beings. There is a strong and warm power, flowing from its strokes and words, which is absolutely impossible to feel from any other person in the world or any writing work that is good at only calligraphy. This is what the great monk Hui Hong of the Song Dynasty said: "The path is great and the morality is profound. It is admired by the Buddhist monastery. Although only a few words and verses, calligraphy's inherent merit in which scholars fight to uncover its mystery, the morality of a master is to be respected." (Calligraphy of Venerable Chao Ran)

Venerable Master Hsing Yun have great compassions in mind. By using calligraphy as a tool to propagate Buddhism work, his calligraphy works have helped him expand the subtle energies so that when people see his writings, they are able to attain Dharma! Therefore, each Venerable Master's handwritten calligraphy treasure is undoubtedly the "incarnation" of the master who not only delights all beings but also makes Dharma widely known. Given these considerations, if you are able to obtain his original handwritten calligraphy work, it should be treasured. If you see a printed version, you can still feel the power of its kindness and eternal protection!

【From One Stroke Calligraphy to the Words After Recovery — See the Power of Compassion】

Fo Guang Yuan Art Gallery Chief Curator
Ven. Ru Chang

Ordinary people learns calligraphy with the belief that it can help with self-cultivation. Those who have excellent calligraphy skills even go on to become artists, like Venerable Master Hong Yi. But many people may wonder why Venerable Master Hsing Yun in his 90s, with shaky hands, mobility difficulties and blurred vision, can still manage to write calligraphy? What is the driving force behind it? What is the motivation?

"Please not look at my writing but look into my heart." This is what Venerable Master Hsing Yun said when "One Stroke Calligraphy" was first exhibited. It was many years later when finally people gradually understood the Master's "heart", a heart of compassion.

In the past, Venerable Master Hsing Yun has expressed that because his eyes could not see clearly, he was unable to read books or the newspaper. Aside from giving lectures or dictating articles, Venerable Master could do nothing but write calligraphy. Due to his poor vision, he must finish writing with one stroke, as so-called "One Stroke Calligraphy" by Venerable Master.

In 2009, in order to enable "Venerable Master Hsing Yun Public Education Trust Fund" to continue supporting social public welfares, he exerted his influence and worked hard raising funds. He even took a step further and launched the "Venerable Master Hsing Yun One Stroke Calligraphy Exhibition". Surprisingly, far beyond everyone's imagination, the power of his "One Stroke Calligraphy" was so tremendously profound and substantial. Up to today, its power still continues!

The hidden energy of "One Stroke Calligraphy" was not achieved overnight. Recalling Venerable Master's footprint of preaching Buddhist Dharma, perhaps it all started from the poster that Venerable Master wrote for Yilan's Leiyin Temple. He then went on to write calligraphy as means to repay the faithful devotees of Pumen Temple in Taipei for their support, which resulted in the establishment of the University of the West. His efforts continued and its merits materialized into the establishment of five universities in four countries: the United States, Taiwan, the Philippines and Australia. In 2009, the funds from "Venerable Master Hsing Yun One Stroke Calligraphy Exhibition" was used to support social welfares such as the "Truthful, Virtuous, and Beautiful Media Awards", the "Hsing Yun Award for Global Chinese Literature", the "Three Acts of Goodness Schools" and "The Hsing Yun Education Award". His efforts even included taking care of young students who were unable to attend school because of poverty in Taiwan, Brazil, the Philippines, India and South Africa. Since 2016, Venerable Master's initiatives through the "Seeds of Hope Project" has been guiding students in to studies or trainings for employment. The power of Venerable Master's brush is evident throughout the world, transcending time and space.

The Venerable Master is always in a wheelchair, writing with his wrist raised, focused and working hard. Bearing the pains from his arms, he continues to write after he was given pain-killer injections. Witnessing the hardship, his disciples worry that the ninety-year-old Venerable Master could no longer take on such work load. However, unexpectedly again,the ninety-year-old Venerable Master began to write long pieces of ancient virtuous, such as Su Dongpo's "Three Verses of Contemplation on Chan", Liu Yuxi's "Inscriptions of a Humble Room", "The Book of Rites-The Great Unity", and even wrote a hundred sentences on "100 Remedies for Life"...What kind of perseverance and transcendence the Venerable Master holds!

At the end of 2016, the Venerable Master had a brain surgery. When his body slightly recovered during the recuperation, the Venerable Master was frequently concerned about the learnings of the students from his "Seeds of Hope Project". He was concerned about their personal growth and future, and he was afraid of any interruptions on their learnings. In order to enable these students to successfully complete their studies,the Venerable Master began working hard again in practicing his calligraphy. The Master stated, "I'm not in pain. I'm not sick. I'm just a little inconvenient." He kept scratching his fingers on his legs to practice writing the words, and after many practices, he used the brush to write on the paper again, which the Master refers to as his "Words After Recovery".

"What else can I do for you?" Many people who come to see the Venerable Master has been shocked by his questioning! A ninety-four-year-old Master in a wheelchair, humbly claimed that he is an old monk himself with still a little compassion to be seen, and yet his compassion is boundless!

The sutra's documentation of the story where the Buddha cuts his flesh to feed the eagles and tigers mirrors what we have also witnessed in the Venerable Master. The compassionate Master provides his body and heart to support all beings. Such support is endless until the visible space ends, the karma of all sentient beings ends, and the worry of all sentient beings ends … the Master's compassionate thoughts toward human beings are continuous without stopping, and so as his tireless body, words and mind. Buddha disciples are always devoted to "dedicating one's body and mind to the world as means to show gratitude to Buddha's grace." The Venerable Master puts this teaching into practice and thoroughly carries it out.

All around the world, the students from "Seeds of Hope Project "often wrote letters to the Venerable Master, asking the Master not to worry about them and assuring him that they are studying hard and will give back to the community, in reciprocity for those who cared about them. Students at Fo Guang Shan Buddhist Centre New Delhi, India always talked about thanking the Venerable Master, because the Venerable Master has not only changed their lives, but even sent them abroad to study at universities in Nanjing, Thailand and Taiwan so that they can see the world. The young girls from the Tianlong team in South Africa, once spoke to the world from the stage at the United Nation, expressing how grateful they are to Venerable Master for changing their lives!

In 2016, a female student from Guang Ming College in the Philippines, in front of more than a thousand young people from dozens of countries around the world, gratefully said to the 90-year-old Venerable Master, "We assure you that in 10 years, all of Guang Ming College graduates will promote Humanistic Buddhism, and I will do my best to contribute to world peace." The Venerable Master responded, "If I don't live until that day, in my afterlife, I'll come back again and see all of you." All those present were so touched and burst into a flood a tears by this dialogue…

From "One Stroke Calligraphy" to the "Words After Recovery", Venerable Master's compassion transcends beyond race and national borders, spreading boundlessly!

〔 *The Aesthetic Philosophy of Venerable Master Hsing Yun* 〕

Fo Guang Yuan Art Gallery Chief Curator
Ven. Ru Chang

No matter where you go in Fo Guang Shan: the Main Shrine, FGS Sutra Repository, or even FGS Buddha Museum, most people will be embraced by the feeling of protection and astonishment by the buildings of Fo Guang Shan.

These feelings come about not from the ingenuity of the buildings' architect but the buildings' portrayal of a broad outlook and unparalleled momentum never before seen in traditional temples. The color tone of the temple's architecture matches the surrounding environment so well that they complement each other. There is no finely crafted or delicate decoration inside the building, on the contrary, every hall harnessed a sacred atmosphere of simplicity but profoundness, purity, and solemness.

It's hard to imagine that these considerations all came from the founder, Venerable Master Hsing Yun, who has no educational background or training in art or architecture. In creating the pure land of the Buddha, it took 50 years of hard work with all his heart and efforts.

Venerable Master's deep comprehension and physical evidence of Buddhism teachings may be appreciated from his writings and lectures. However, many people are often curious about how the Venerable Master can build the temple so beautifully and how did he possibly come up with the idea of establishing an art gallery in a temple. Moreover, how was he able to preserve the Buddhist culture in contemporary buildings while combining tradition and modernity so harmoniously? And even, all artists agreed that Venerable Master Hsing Yun indeed knows art very well and that he could be regarded as their peers.

Being born during wartime and growing up in poverty when even getting food was very difficult, never been to school in his entire life and became a monk at the age of twelve, we often wonder how did Venerable Master Hsing Yun obtain his sense of aesthetics?

Usually, people can see the aesthetic connotation of the founder from the temple's architecture. This connotation is related to one's cultivation and literacy as well as one's experience and accumulation in Buddhism, culture, and art. Therefore, to understand the aesthetic ideas of Venerable Master Hsing Yun, perhaps it may be worthwhile for us to examine these following aspects.

"There was a stone Buddhist grotto with a carved Buddha on the mountain when I was a little monk at Qixia Shan Temple. We could even play hide and seek in the ear of the largest infinite carved Amitayus Buddha. These many stone carvings which lasted hundred thousand years held thousands of stories within. Therefore, Buddhist art has become an important part of my life since then," written by Venerable Master Hsing Yun in the "Buddhist Affinities Across 100 Years." Besides, he also visited many major caves in mainland China, such as Dunhuang, Yungang, Longmen, etc. From an aesthetic point of view, the cave is the best way to show the beauty of Buddhist art. Buddhist art from varying time frames such as the inscriptions on precipices and the mural painting of Dunhuang have perhaps unknowingly helped in cultivating Venerable Master Hsing Yun's artistic creativity with regards to Buddha statues.

During studies at the Jiaoshan Buddhist College of Dinghui Temple in Zhenjiang, there were many profound enlightenments for the Venerable Master, especially in the cultivation of literature and aesthetics. The Master even stated that if it's not for Jiaoshan Buddhist College, there would be no Hsing Yun today. Dinghui Temple is surrounded by the Yangtze River and there exist dozens of auxiliary temples in the area, all of which have galleries or studios in them. "When I was 18 or 19 years old, I knew little about everything, so as long as I had time, I would go to the studio/gallery to enjoy the artworks and try to learn more." As such, it can be concluded that Venerable Master Hsin Yun's impeccable taste in art has its origins. His appreciation for the beauty in literature and calligraphy inspired his ideal of propagating Buddhism from cultural perspectives.

In fact, the Venerable Master's aestheticism spanned broadly. In the "Buddhism Series - Use of the Teachings" written by the Venerable Master in early years, he wrote articles explaining the relationship between Buddhism and each kind of aesthetic arts, such as calligraphy, tea ceremony, flower arrangement, and even craft, sculpture, painting, architecture, as well as music, dance, drama, literature, etc... If you read these articles carefully, you will discover the origins behind the Venerable Master's aestheticism to be so extensive and profound.

In addition to the above-mentioned experiences, the Venerable Master also received inspirations from the sutras. In the "Mulasarvastivadavinayakṣudra kavastu", after an Anathapiṇḍada elder gave a garden to Buddha, he said, "If I don't paint in color painting, it will not be dignified. If Buddha shall allow me, I will decorate it." So Anathapiṇḍada elders went to ask Buddha, and Buddha said, "As you wish for it be become a painting."

Venerable Master indicated that we could learn from this paragraph of the sutra that there were four main purposes of paintings during the Buddha era:

1. To make the temple solemn;

2. To preach the Dharma;

3. To praise the Buddha's ethics;

4. To acquire affinity of cultivation.

These may perhaps be the main reasons why the Venerable Master is committed to the development of Buddhism aesthetics.

The period of learning Buddhism in mainland China marked the progressional development of Master Hsing Yun's aesthetic philosophy. After coming to Taiwan, he began having an affinity toward building temples. Thereby, the Venerable Master's specific insights on aesthetics were put into practice in the process of the temple's construction.

The architectural aesthetics of Venerable Master Hsing Yun is evident even in the early days of founding Fo Guang Shan. More than fifty years ago, facing the desolate mountain full of wild grass and bamboo, the Venerable Master had already begun to conceive the blueprint for the future of Fo Guang Shan.

At that time, the Venerable Master asked Mr. Xie Runde, an engineer at CPC Corporation, to draw a panorama sketch of Fo Guang Shan. Details of the buildings from the color to the configuration all resonated with Venerable Master's philosophy on the aesthetics of a temple. Comparing the original sketch to present-day Fo Guang Shan 50 years later, it looked almost identical. After the completion of the majestic temple of Fo Guang Shan, not only did it provide guidance to more believers, it also attracted countless visitors. We could not help but admire the Venerable Master's unique sense of aesthetics and vision.

"The Great Buddha" at Fo Guang Shan and the "Fo Guang Big Buddha" at the Buddha Museum are now the landmarks of Fo Guang Shan. Whenever one walks into the Main Shrine or Great Compassion Shrine, one can find that the Venerable Master presents the mural paintings and statue of the grottoes in the halls one by one. Entering the shrine is like entering the Dunhuang Grottoes.

During the process of building the temple, the Venerable Master thought: What would the temple become if there were not even a piece of calligraphy or painting that could inspire people to be kind? What would this temple be if there was no culture within? In the early days, many artists donated their works to the Venerable Master for setting up schools and building monasteries. The Venerable Master treasured all the calligraphy and paintings, and even made a vow to build a museum comparable to the National Palace Museum in the future.

How does the Venerable Master consider the importance of having an art gallery in a temple? Since the Venerable Master's establishment of the Fo Guang Shan Cultural Exhibition Hall (later renamed as the Museum of Buddhist Treasures) in 1983, exhibition halls have been set up in major Fo Guang Shan branches both in Taiwan and overseas. In Fo Guang Shan's main headquarter, the gallery is located just behind the Main Shrine.

In 1994, as an effort to raise funds for the establishment of Fo Guang University, "Fo Guang Yuan Art Gallery" was formally established. Presently, there are 27 such galleries around the world. Visitors include artists, calligraphers, musicians, educators, school principals, teachers, children, etc.

The Venerable Master once said, "Say good words, good words mean speaking the truth; Do good deeds, good deeds mean good behavior; Think good thoughts, good thoughts mean aesthetics, having a beautiful heart." Venerable Master Hsing Yun's aesthetic ideals are formed from inside out. Likewise to what he said with regards to his one-stroke calligraphy, "Please look beyond my writings, look into my heart." His aesthetic philosophy bestowed upon Fo Guang Shan its astounding beauty. From the color tone, building configuration, to the traffic flow of the temple, everything was designed to make people feel at ease and comfortable.

In the "Avatamsake Sutra", it states, "All is but a creation of the mind." Canonical Text of Mere-Representation also said, "The three realms are only mind, and all things are consciousness." Fo Guang Shan, founded by Venerable Master Hsing Yun, is an exemplary epitome of the Master's "mind", a "mind" full of compassion for all beings. At last, we have discovered that the aesthetic ideals of Venerable Master Hsing Yun is nonetheless the intrinsic principles of Humanistic Buddhism.

VIII • Selections of "Venerable Master Hsing Yun's One-Stroke Calligraphy"

〖 *Don't Look at My Writing, Please Look at My Heart* 〗

I lived in Taiwan Yilan for twenty-six years. Every year I would write a slogan throughout the twenty-six years of the Seven-day Amitabha Chanting Retreat. As I realized I did not practice regularly, there were no improvements. I feel that in my life, I have three shortcomings: 1) I am from Yangzhou of Jiangsu province. So, my native accent unto today cannot be changed. Numerous times I have attempted to learn English and Japanese, each time without success. 2) I cannot sing. I cannot sing Buddhist chants well. I am absolutely shameful about it as I am a monk. 3) I am not good at writing because I do not have confidence in myself. Thus, I always tell others not to look at just my writing, but to look for my heart in these writings. For me, I feel that at least I have a bit of compassion that I can show you.

(An excerpt from Venerable Master Hsing Yun's "Origin of One-Stroke Calligraphy")

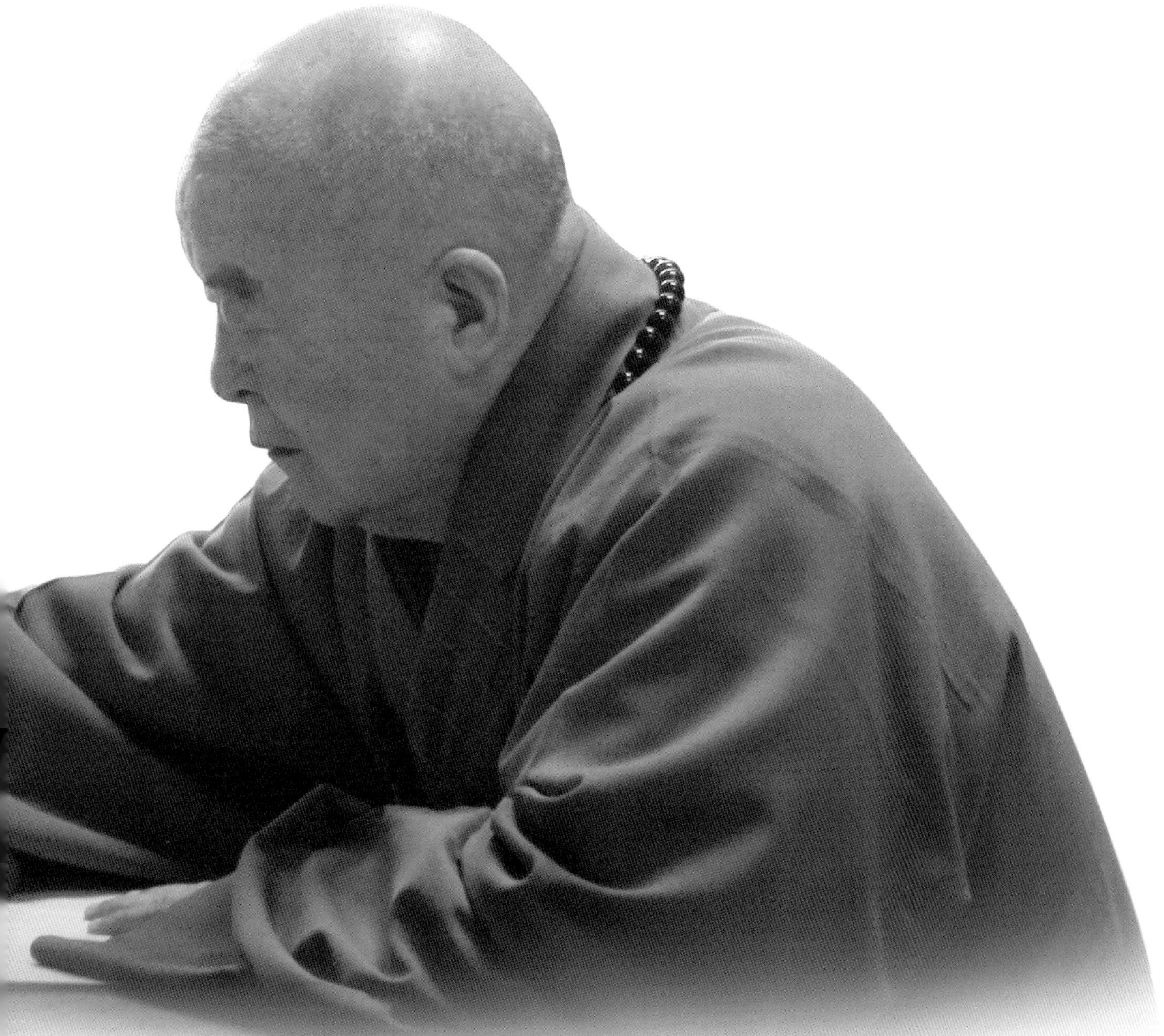

【 *What Is One-Stroke Calligraphy* 】

At 94 years of age, Venerable Master Hsing Yun's eyes have deteriorated due to his diabetic condition, which was diagnosed over 40 years ago. Barely able to see, each of his calligraphy work was completed in one stroke without stopping. If he stopped, he would be unable to position his next stroke and, therefore, would be unable to complete it. He relies on his mind's eye and his "Dharma eye" by dipping the brush into the ink and immediately writing the words in one stroke, thus giving his work its name, 'One-Stroke Calligraphy.' Venerable Master Hsing Yun said, "Writing in one stroke without stopping is similar to the way I handle everything in life, which is to move forward courageously, without any hesitation."

一筆一字

星雲

华严经偈

二〇二二年六月

常乐要柔和
忍辱为法
内怀慈悲
志无怯弱

佛光山 □□ 書

Hua Yan Jing Ji
Chang Le Rou He Ren Ru Fa
An Zhu Ci Bei Xi She Zhong

Find Joy in Being Gentle and Patient Abide Peacefully in Kindness, Compassion, Joy, and Equanimity
Where the body and mind abide.

華嚴經偈
常樂柔和忍辱法
安住慈悲喜捨中

身心的安住處。

千江有水千江月
萬里無雲萬里天

Qian Jiang You Shui Qian Jiang Yue
Wan Li Wu Yun Wan Li Tian

The Moon is Reflected in a Thousand Rivers
Without Clouds the Sky is Vast

Be like the illuminating moon reflected in the water everywhere to help relieve beings from suffering.

No defilements nor worries like a cloudless and clear sky.

千江有水千江月
萬里無雲萬里天

如水中月隨處映現，助人離苦。
如無雲晴空，無煩無惱。

難忍能忍

Nan Ren Neng Ren

Tolerating the Intolerable
Endure what others find intolerable.

難忍能忍
忍人所不能忍。

雲水三千

星雲

Yun Shui San Qian

Cloud and Water
A symbol of freedom.

雲水三千
象徵自由。

生死忍

Sheng Ren Fa Ren

Ordinary Tolerance and Dharma Tolerance
The persisting strength to survive in this world and
power to transform defilements into wisdom.

生忍法忍

生存在世間的耐力和轉煩惱為智慧的力量。

心為大海

Xin Ru Da Hai

A Mind as Great as the Ocean
A broad and generous mind.

心如大海
心量廣大。

不忘初心

Bu Wang Chu Xin

Never Forget One's Initial Aspirations
Preserve one's initial intentions.

不忘初心
保持初衷。

十全十美

Shi Quan Shi Mei

Perfect in Every Way
A perfect outcome for all good things.

十全十美
一切好事圓滿。

久佛初見

Ru Fo Zhi Jian

Entering the View of the Buddha
Share the same thoughts as the Buddha.

入佛知見

和佛陀同樣的想法。

一心不二

Yi Xin Bu Er

Wholeheartedly

Do not constantly change your mind.

一心不二

不要三心二意。

觀自在

Guan Zi Zai

Avalokitesvara
Liberation and happiness.

觀自在
解脫快樂。

清月人舍

Fa Tong She

Dharma Abode
See the Dharma as your home.

法同舍

以佛法為家。

撲無貝

Pu Shi

Down-to-Earth
Be realistic and unexaggerating.

樸實
實在不浮誇。

茶禅

Cha Chan

Tea Chan
The way of Chan in tea drinking.

茶禪

茶中的禪道。

佐道

Wu Dao

Awaken to the Path
Realize the Truth.

悟道
證悟真理。

放下

Fang Xia

Let Go

Carry no burdens in our mind.

放下
心中不要有負擔。

行佛

Xing Fo

Practice the Buddha's Way
Practice what the Buddha practiced.

行佛

行佛之所行。

中道

Zhong Dao

Middle Way
Unbiased.

中道
不偏不倚。

禅

Chan

Chan
The mind inherent in everyone.

禪

每個人的自心。

静

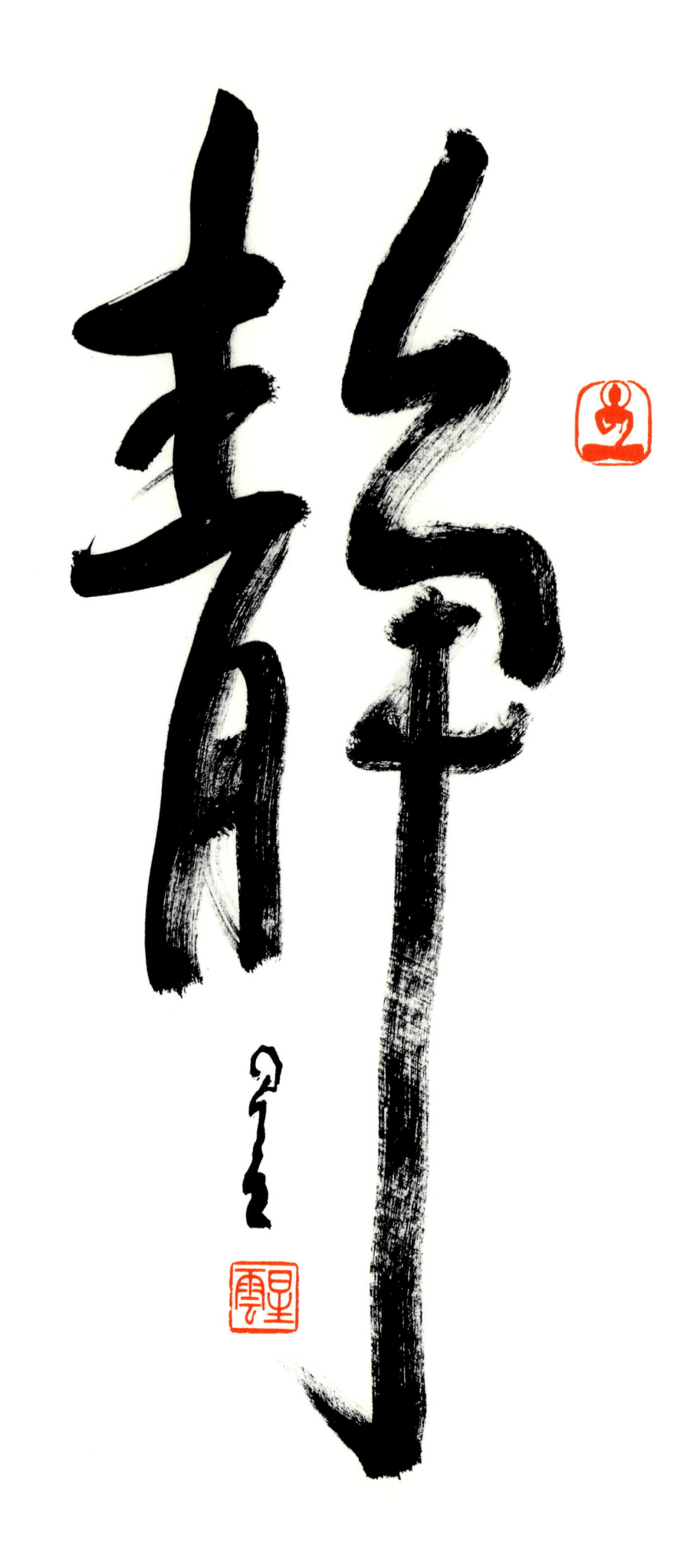

Jing

Stillness

Do not be affected by the external world.

靜
不隨外境動搖。

佛

Fo

Buddha
The Awakened One.

佛
覺
者
。

一筆了事

【何謂一筆字書法】

九十四歲的星雲大師，由於四十多年的糖尿病，導致視網膜剝離，合併眼底黃斑部細胞鈣化，雙眼視力模糊，幾乎看不見。

所以他的每一幅書法作品都是「一筆」到底，因為只要中途停頓，就會看不清、抓不準筆畫而難以下筆。

憑藉「心眼」與「法眼」，成就沾墨落筆一揮而就的書法，稱為「一筆字」。

大師自己表示：「寫字一筆到底，如同我這一生做任何事秉持勇往向前，毫不猶豫的態度。」

【不要看我的字，請看我的心】

我在台灣宜蘭連續住了二十六年，二十六年的「佛七法會」，我每一年都要寫一次標語，自覺平常並沒有練習，所以沒有進步。

我覺得我這一生有三個缺點：

第一，我是江蘇揚州人，鄉音腔調至今改不了，尤其學過多次的英文、日語，都沒有成功；

第二，我不會唱歌，梵唄唱誦不好，實在愧對作為一個出家人；

第三，不會寫字，因此就沒有信心。

所以我後來經常對人說，你們不可以看我的字，但可以看我的心，因為我心裡還有一點慈悲心，可以給你們看。

摘自星雲大師〈一筆字的因緣〉

捌・〈星雲大師一筆字書法〉選輯

妙因缘

【覺有情——星雲大師墨跡世界巡迴展】

二〇〇八・紐西蘭北島佛光緣美術館

二〇〇七・中國南京博物館
重慶中國三峽博物館
中國無錫市體育館
中國揚州博物館
香港大學美術博物館
紐西蘭北島佛光山

二〇〇六・澳洲昆士蘭演藝中心
中國湖南省博物館
香港中央圖書館
臺灣屏東文化中心
臺灣臺北國父紀念館
臺灣佛光緣美術館總館

二〇〇五・美國柏克萊大學
美國西來大學
馬來西亞國家畫廊

44

二〇一四
- 中國上海中華藝術宮
- 中國廣西省壯族自治區博物館
- 中國遼寧省覺華島
- 中國浙江美術館館
- 中國山東博物館
- 中國大連現代博物館
- 中國鎮江博物館
- 中國閩台緣博物館
- 中國廈門市博物館

二〇一三
- 中國國家博物館
- 中國雲南省博物館
- 中國廣東省博物館
- 中國西安博物院
- 中國甘肅省博物館
- 中國山西太原美術館
- 中國內蒙古博物院

- 中國河南博物院
- 中國湖北省博物館
- 中國湖州市博物館
- 中國奉化雪竇山資聖禪寺
- 中國南京大學星雲樓
- 日本山梨縣立圖書館
- 臺灣臺北一〇一景觀台
- 臺灣高雄佛光山雲居樓

二〇〇九
- 新加坡佛光山
- 馬來西亞佛光緣美術館東禪館
- 臺灣佛光緣美術館總館
- 臺灣佛光緣美術館臺北館

- 臺灣嘉義市政府
- 臺灣佛光緣美術館宜蘭館
- 臺灣佛光緣美術館臺中館
- 臺灣佛光緣美術館臺南館
- 臺灣佛光緣美術館高雄館

二〇一五
- 中國蘇州嘉應會館美術館
- 澳門理工學院
- 香港佛光緣美術館
- 日本名古屋市博物館
- 日本福岡市美術館
- 日本東京藝術劇場
- 日本神奈川縣民會館本館
- 日本群馬縣民會館
- 日本大阪六軒茶屋展覽廳
- 日本山梨縣立圖書館
- 日本大阪佛光山寺
- 臺灣高雄佛光山佛陀紀念館
- 臺灣佛光緣美術館總館
- 臺灣佛光緣美術館屏東館
- 臺灣佛光緣美術館臺南館
- 臺灣佛光緣美術館彰化館
- 臺灣佛光緣美術館臺中館
- 臺灣佛光緣美術館臺北館
- 臺灣佛光緣美術館宜蘭館
- 臺灣高雄佛光山藏經樓
- 臺灣佛光山月光寺
- 臺灣佛光山竹東大覺寺
- 義大利米蘭世博中國館
- 中國安徽博物院
- 中國蘇州博物館
- 中國寧波美術館

二〇一三
- 中國天津美術館
- 中國海南省博物館
- 法國巴黎佛光緣美術館
- 馬來西亞柔佛巴魯五福城（MY 圖書館）
- 菲律賓達沃市博物館
- 菲律賓佛光山萬年寺
- 紐西蘭北島佛光緣美術館
- 加拿大多倫多佛光山寶藏館
- 澳洲墨爾本佛光緣美術館
- 臺灣臺北國立歷史博物館
- 加拿大多倫多懷雅遜大學羅渣士管理學院

二〇一二
- 國立丹麥博物館
- 瑞典斯德哥爾摩東方博物館
- 澳洲達令港中國花園
- 日本寶塚市立國際文化中心

二〇一〇
- 奧地利維也納阿爾貝蒂娜博物館
- 奧地利維也納聯合國國際中心
- 北京中國美術館
- 香港佛光緣美術館
- 日本京都佛教大學四條文教中心
- 日本東京佛光山寺
- 日本東京橫濱三溪園
- 臺灣臺北國父紀念館

攝影 蔡榮豐

荷蘭佛光山荷華寺
美國德州首府州議會大廳
美國佛州橘郡會議大廈 Atrium 畫廊
美國聖地牙哥華人歷史博物館
美國加州州立大學（沙加緬度）圖書館藝術展覽館
美國邁阿密佛光山
美國曼城佛光山
阿根廷佛光山
巴拉圭佛光山禪淨中心
加拿大多倫多佛光山
加拿大溫哥華佛光山
澳洲佛光山中天寺
澳洲墨爾本佛光緣美術館
澳洲南島佛光緣美術館
紐西蘭南島佛光緣美術館
紐西蘭北島佛光緣美術館
新加坡佛光山
馬來西亞佛光緣美術館東禪館
菲律賓佛光緣美術館馬尼拉館
中國國家博物館
中國南京博物院
中國河北省博物院
中國重慶美術館
中國宜興市博物館
中國揚州美術館
中國宜興大覺寺美術館
中國上海星雲文教館美術館

【星雲大師 一筆字書法展展歷】

二〇一九・美國紐約林肯中心 David H. Kock

二〇一八・布魯塞爾歐洲議會大廈
葡萄牙里斯本東方博物館
中國貴州美術館
中國江蘇常州溧陽市博物館
日本山梨縣立美術館

二〇一七・美國佛州布羅瓦郡圖書總館
臺灣桃園市政府
臺灣南華大學
臺灣暨南國際大學圖書館

二〇一六・法國巴黎第十三區市政廳
法國巴黎佛光緣美術館
佛光山日內瓦會議中心
丹麥哥本哈根市政廳
英國倫敦亞洲之家
德國柏林佛光山
奧地利維也納佛光山
比利時佛光山
瑞士佛光山

三界唯心

不禁令人讚歎大師的獨到的美學與遠見。

佛光山的「接引大佛」與佛館的「佛光大佛」，如今都成為佛光山的地標。而無論走進大雄寶殿或大悲殿，都可發現，大師將石窟的繪畫與造像藝術一一呈現在殿堂裡，走進大殿，就如同走進敦煌石窟。

在建寺的過程，大師思考：如果寺廟裡連一張勸人向善的字畫都沒有，這寺廟沒有文化，還能算什麼呢？早期許多藝術家將作品捐贈給大師辦學建寺，大師將所有捐贈的字畫收藏起來，甚至發願，將來要蓋一個媲美故宮的博物館。

大師是如何地重視道場裡需要有美術館。從一九八三年大師成立佛光山文物陳列館（後更名寶藏館）開始，在海內外主要道場都設置有展覽館。在總本山，大師更將展覽館就直接設在大雄寶殿的正後方。

一九九四年，為籌措佛光大學建校基金，正式成立「佛光緣美術館」，及至目前，全世界已有二十七個美術館。來到佛光山的訪客，有藝術家、書法家、音樂家、教育家、學校的校長、老師與小朋友等等。

大師說：「口說好話，好話就是真話；身做好事，好事就是善事；心存好念，好念就是美學，就是美心。」星雲大師的美學思想，成於內而形於外，如同大師寫一筆字所強調：「請不要看我的字，可以看我的心。」他的美學思想，成就了今天讓人驚豔的佛光山之美，從顏色基調、房子配置、往來動線上，總是讓人感到自在愉悅。

《華嚴經》云：「一切唯心造。」唯識典籍言：「三界唯心，萬法唯識。」星雲大師所創建的佛光山，實則呈現的就是大師的「心」，一顆充滿慈悲、只為眾生的「心」。至此，我們可以發現，星雲大師的美學思想，就是大師人間佛教的思想。

窟，如：敦煌、雲岡、龍門等。從美學的角度來看，石窟，是最能展現佛教藝術在佛像造像上的創造力。

在鎮江定慧寺焦山佛學院學習期間，對大師更有許多深刻的啟蒙，尤其在文學與美學養成上，大師甚至表示，沒有焦山佛學院就沒有今天的星雲。四周環繞著長江的定慧寺，其前後左右有數十間附屬庵堂，這些庵堂都設有畫廊或畫室。大師描述：「在我十八、九歲的時候還很孤陋寡聞，因此只要有時間，就會跑到他們的畫室畫廊去欣賞觀摩。」由此可知，大師對繪畫的鑑賞力是其來有自的。文學之美與字畫之美，這些經驗開始啟發大師以文化弘法度眾的理想。

實際上大師的美學思想含攝範圍甚為廣泛。在大師早期所寫的《佛教》叢書，其中《教用》一冊裡就將各種美學藝術，如：書法、茶道、花道、乃至工藝、雕塑、繪畫、建築、甚至音樂、舞蹈、戲劇、文學等等，寫成一篇篇的專文，闡述佛教與這些藝術的關係。細細閱讀這些文章即可發現，原來大師的美學思想是這麼的廣博與深入。

除了上述的種種經驗外，大師也從經典上獲得啟發。在《根本說一切有部毗奈耶雜事》卷十七說：「給孤長者施園之後，作如是念：『若不彩畫，便不端嚴。佛若許者，我欲裝飾。』即往白佛，佛言：『隨意當畫』……」大師表示：「從這段經文記載可知，佛陀時期的繪畫有四個目的：一、莊嚴寺院道場；二、宣揚佛陀教法；三、顯揚佛陀聖德；四、增益修道因緣。」這或許正是大師致力於佛教美學發展的主因。

在大陸參學時期，可說是星雲大師美學思想的養成期，來到台灣後，開始有了建寺因緣，於是大師的美學思想在建寺過程中，有了具體實踐。

星雲大師的建築美學始見於佛光山開山初期。五十多年前，面對滿是野草刺竹的一塊荒山，大師就開始構思未來佛光山的藍圖。

當時，大師找了任職中油工程師的謝潤德居士，繪製了一幅「未來佛光山」的全景圖。從顏色到建築配置，都呈現出當時大師對寺廟美學的思想。現在拿來對照五十年後建成的佛光山，幾乎是一模一樣。佛光山這座莊嚴無比的道場完成後，不僅接引更多的信徒，連觀光客竟也絡繹不絕，

認識星雲大師的美學思想

佛光緣美術館總館館長 釋如常

第一次到佛光山的訪客，無論是走到大雄寶殿，或是藏經樓，乃至佛陀紀念館，多數人對佛光山的建築群都會感到攝受與震撼。

這樣的覺受，並非佛光山的建築有多麼的標新立異，讓訪客訝異的是，在傳統寺廟建築上，看見一種前所未有的開闊視野與氣勢；在寺廟建築色彩基調上，與周遭環境彼此是如此的契合與相得益彰。走進建築內部，沒有所謂的精雕細琢或金碧輝煌；相反的，所有的殿堂都呈現一股樸實與深邃、清淨與莊嚴的神聖氛圍。

大家很難想像，這些全來自不曾受過任何藝術或是建築訓練的佛光山開山─星雲大師以五十年的歲月一手擘劃所打造出來的佛國淨土！

家師在佛教思想上的深入與體證，一般人或可從大師的著作與講演上領略一二。但許多人好奇的是：大師怎麼可以把寺廟蓋得這麼美？怎麼知道要在寺廟設置美術館？又如何將現代建築保留佛教文化，將傳統和現代結合得如此和諧；乃至，藝術家也都覺得大師很懂藝術，是他們的知己！

生長在一個戰亂與貧窮，連吃飯都成問題的年代，一輩子沒上過學校，十二歲就出家，究竟星雲大師的美學思想啟蒙於何處？

一般人從寺廟建築可以看出一個開山祖師的美學內涵，這內涵，實則與一個人的修持與素養相關，其含攝佛學及文化藝術上的經驗與積累。因此，要理解星雲大師的美學思想，或許可從這幾方面來探討。

在《百年佛緣》中，大師寫到：「我自己年幼出家的棲霞山寺，山上就有一個石刻的千佛洞，最大的無量壽佛，我們還可以躲到他耳朵裡面去捉迷藏。這許多石刻，歷經百千年，有千百個故事，因此，佛教藝術也成為我成長生命裡重要的一部分。」此外，大師也曾參訪中國大陸各大石大師竟從九十歲起開始寫長篇的古德偈語，如蘇東坡的〈參禪三偈〉，劉禹錫的〈陋室銘〉、《禮記·禮運大同篇》，甚至寫出一百句的「對治百法」……這又是何等的堅忍與超越！

二○一六年底大師腦部手術，休養中的大師在身體稍稍恢復時，又頻頻關心關心他們的成長與未來，深怕好苗子的學習中斷。為了讓各地的好苗子能夠順利完成學業，又隨即開始勤奮努力練字。大師說：「我沒有痛苦，我沒有生病，只是有點不方便。」他以手指不斷地在自己的腿上比劃揣摩，及至熟練後，再次提筆書寫，此時大師稱之為「病後字」。

「我還可以為您做什麼？」許多人來見大師，都曾被大師的這句話震懾！一位九十四歲坐著輪椅，謙稱自己還有一點慈悲心可以給人看的老和尚，那一點慈悲是何等的無量無邊！

經典記載佛陀所說的割肉餵鷹、捨身飼虎的故事，彷彿我們也在大師的身上親眼目睹。那是大師為眾生以身心為供養的慈悲，這樣的供養無窮無盡，直至虛空界盡、眾生業盡、眾生煩惱盡……是大師念念相續無有間斷，身語意業無有疲厭的慈悲。佛弟子總是發願「將此身心奉塵剎，是則名為報佛恩」，星雲大師則是信受奉行，徹底實踐。

二○一六年，菲律賓光明大學一位女同學為感謝大師的恩澤，當著數十個國家一千多名青年的面前，對九十歲的星雲大師說道：「我們向您保證，十年後，所有光明大學的畢業生都會弘揚人間佛教，而我將傾盡所學，為世界和平努力。」大師則回應：「如果我活不到那天，來世，我會再回來看您們。」一席對話，感動全場無數的人，淚如雨下……

世界各地的好苗子常常寫信給大師，要大師放心，他們會努力讀書，將來回饋社會，以報答關心他們的人。印度佛光山沙彌學園的學生總是將感謝師公的話掛在嘴邊，因為師公不僅改變他們的生命，甚至送他們出國到南京、到泰國、到台灣就讀大學，讓他們看見這個世界；而遠在南非的天龍隊年輕女孩，則走進聯合國舞台向全世界的人說：感謝星雲大師翻轉她們的生命！

一筆字到病後字，大師的慈悲，跨越種族、沒有國界，無遠弗屆！

【一筆字到病後字——看見慈悲的力量】
佛光緣美術館總館長　釋如常

一般人學習書法認為可以修身養性，書藝佳者甚至發展成為藝術；在佛門則為修持的法門之一，更進一步則是弘道傳法，如弘一大師即是。但很多人可能會好奇，手抖、行動不便、眼睛看不見、九十幾歲的星雲大師為什麼還要寫書法？這背後究竟是什麼動力驅使？動機又為何？

猶記星雲大師在開始展出一筆字時便說：「請不要看我的字，請看我的心。」在多年之後，終於有人逐漸理解，看懂了大師的「心」，一顆慈悲的心。

大師過去曾表示自己因為眼睛看不清楚，不能看書，也不能看報紙，在課徒、口述文章之餘，只好寫書法。因為看不清楚，必須一筆到底，大師便稱為「一筆字」。

二○○九年，為讓「公益信託星雲大師教育基金」能持續支持社會公益，發揮影響力，積極籌措基金善款，更開啟了「星雲大師一筆字書法展」的因緣。然而，遠遠超乎大家所想像的，一筆字的力量竟如此的深遠巨大，及至今日仍持續未歇！

一筆字所潛藏的能量，非一夕所成，回溯大師的弘法足跡，或許應該從大師為宜蘭雷音寺所寫的招貼紙開始醞釀起，進而在台北普門寺為答謝信徒的供養，竟寫出一所西來大學，乃至陸續寫出目前在美國、台灣、菲律賓、澳洲等共四個國家的五所大學。二○○九年更以「星雲大師一筆字書法展」善款支持「星雲真善美新聞傳播獎」、「全球華文文學星雲獎」、「三好校園實踐學校」、「星雲教育獎」等社會公益；最後甚至開始照顧台灣、巴西、菲律賓、印度以及南非等因為貧窮無法就學的青年學子，二○一六年起以「好苗子計畫」輔導就學就業。大師這一支筆的力量橫遍十方，超越時間與空間。

大師總是坐著輪椅，懸腕而寫，專注努力勤奮，即便手臂疼痛不已仍強忍著，打完止痛針繼續寫。徒眾看了難免憂心不捨，唯恐已屆九十高齡的師父不堪負荷；然而，再次出乎大家意料的，筆者認為在這一點上，星雲大師書寫的動機就大為不同，首先，以大師推動「人間佛教」與「生活佛教」的性格，其生活與行程的緊湊，非弘一當年的出家生活所能想像，既沒有時間練字，而且自己也認為寫的字不好看。所以大師的寫字目的較之弘一法師更為純綷，他完全不是為了自己，相反的，大師純綷是為了要「給人歡喜」，才給信徒們寫字，同時，大師也瞭解，藉由他加持的文字，也能協助信徒們「同趣佛道」！

古人說：「書者，如也，如其人，如其情。」也就是說書法雖然是文字，但與印刷出來的冷冰冰的文字全然不同，它雖是無聲的，但是：「觀書如觀人」，見到一個人手寫的書跡，你就感受到書寫者打破時空的距離活生生地再現在你眼前。古人所謂：「千里書疏，如同覿面」。這不但在沒有人像攝影的古代，對眾生盈盈的加持和諄諄的教誨，有一股強大而溫暖的力量，從其筆劃和文字中湧出，覺上遠比電子信件親切得多，如同親見其人一般。

就是這一層道理，大師的信徒們，都渴望擁有大師親書的墨寶手跡，因為從大師的墨寶中，大師既莊嚴又慈悲可親的相貌和精神立即浮現在觀者的眼前，而且大師在書寫每件作品時，對選句的內容，都是「揣摩醞釀，然後小心下筆」，並且「多一分祝願」，因此令觀者感受到大師集一生的修為，對眾生盈盈的加持和諄諄的教誨，有一股強大而溫暖的力量，從其筆劃和文字中湧出，這是絕對無法從世間任何另一個人或任一件只以書藝擅長的書跡作品中所能感受得到的！這也就是宋代高僧惠洪所說的：「道大德博，為叢林所宗仰，雖其片言只偈，翰墨遊戲，學者爭秘之，尊其道師之德耳。」（題釋昭然墨寶）

星雲大師以「大慈過人」的心胸，「以書法為佛事」，留下這些墨寶來助其擴大潛移默化的能量，使人觀其字即得佛法！因此每一幅大師的手跡墨寶，無疑是既令眾生歡喜又令佛法廣被的大師的「分身」。是以，能得大師親筆墨寶的固然應珍之如同拱璧，即使是見到印刷品也能感受其慈雲永護的力量！

柒・以翰墨為佛事

【星雲大師以書法為佛事】　臺灣大學藝術史研究所教授　傅申

書法藝術的媒體是文字，故此一特殊藝術必定產生於知識份子的階層，而佛門的大德高僧，亦必定是智識份子中的精英人物，是以歷代的高僧不但為我們留下了許多法語和禪詩，而且因為毛筆是古人唯一的書寫工具，所以也留下了許多寶貴的墨寶。

筆者在為《明清近代高僧書法展》一書作序：〈以翰墨為佛事〉一文中歷數隋唐以來高僧所留下的墨蹟，書寫者雖然距今數百年甚至上千年，然而透過他們的一筆一畫，卻將他們度世弘法的願力深深烙印在每一位觀者的內心深處。

出生於二十世紀初戰亂時期的星雲大師則迥然不同於史上眾多善書高僧，因為他從年輕時就忙於學佛修行，接著是忙於弘法利生，所以他自己說：「哪有時間練字？！」

因此不像弘一法師在出家前就有機會練習書法：「居俗之日，嘗好臨寫碑帖，積久盈尺。」待弘一出家之後仍然樂此不疲，故曾自省曰：「夫耽樂書術，增長放逸，佛所深戒。」也就是說，如果只是為了喜歡寫字而寫字，對佛家來說，並不值得提倡。但是弘一發現了「以翰墨為佛事」的作用：「然研習之者能盡其美，以是書寫佛典，流傳於世，令諸眾生歡喜受持。自利利他，同趣佛道，非無益矣。」可見弘一法師的書寫佛典，原是由於他個人的興趣所好，而且他造詣很高，能盡其美，因此他的書法既能「令諸眾生歡喜受持」，又能使眾生「同趣佛道」！

- 步驟四：
將清水慢慢加入石膏粉中（水量約七分），水與石膏粉攪拌，感覺不太稀也不太濃，如優酪乳就可以了。〔圖3〕

- 步驟五：
將攪拌好的石膏漿倒入石頭形狀的陶土杯中，要全倒滿，如〔圖4〕。石膏漿表面因為空氣關係，會冒出小泡泡，可輕輕將盛滿石膏漿的陶土於桌面上敲一敲，小泡泡就會不見了。

- 步驟六：
將小片珍珠版（要比陶土杯大）蓋在陶土嘴巴，不讓石膏漿流出來，〔圖5〕。之後慢慢倒反，珍珠版朝下〔圖6〕。此刻石膏漿會慢慢發熱，不用擔心。等待約十五分鐘，石膏漿將會變成硬石膏了。

- 步驟七：
石膏硬後，就可以將陶土撥開，如石頭狀的印章可以開始篆刻了。（若石膏的表面不夠平滑，或很多小洞洞，可以用砂紙磨一磨。）若要刻文字，記得要刻反字，〔圖7〕因為蓋章時才會變成正字。（可以先將文字寫在薄紙，將薄紙翻過來便是反字。依照反字的形狀用鉛筆刻在石膏的表面上。要刻深，才可以印出圖案）。

- 步驟八：
自己做印泥。用紅色顏料加一點黑色顏料攪拌成暗紅色，用薄海綿吸取顏料，便可以將印章沾顏料蓋印了。

陸・創意印章

為自己、朋友、家人來個快速印章製作，只需要三十分鐘就可以了。大人小孩都可以自己動手做喔！

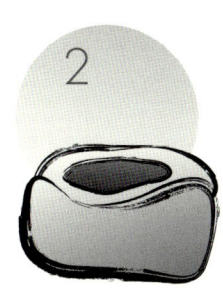

【準備材料】

隨地撿到的石頭一個（可選擇造型奇特，形狀大小約五至十公分）紙黏土一包或使用陶土（可回收再使用）、小紙杯、石膏粉（半紙杯）、清水、鉛筆、小片珍珠版、廣告顏料（紅、黑）、薄海綿一片。

- 步驟一：
做印章模子：將石頭以陶土或紙黏土包一半，底下不可以穿洞喔。〔圖1〕

- 步驟二：
將陶土輕輕拔開，陶土就猶如小茶杯可以盛水。〔圖2〕

- 步驟三：
將石膏粉放入紙杯中，約半杯。

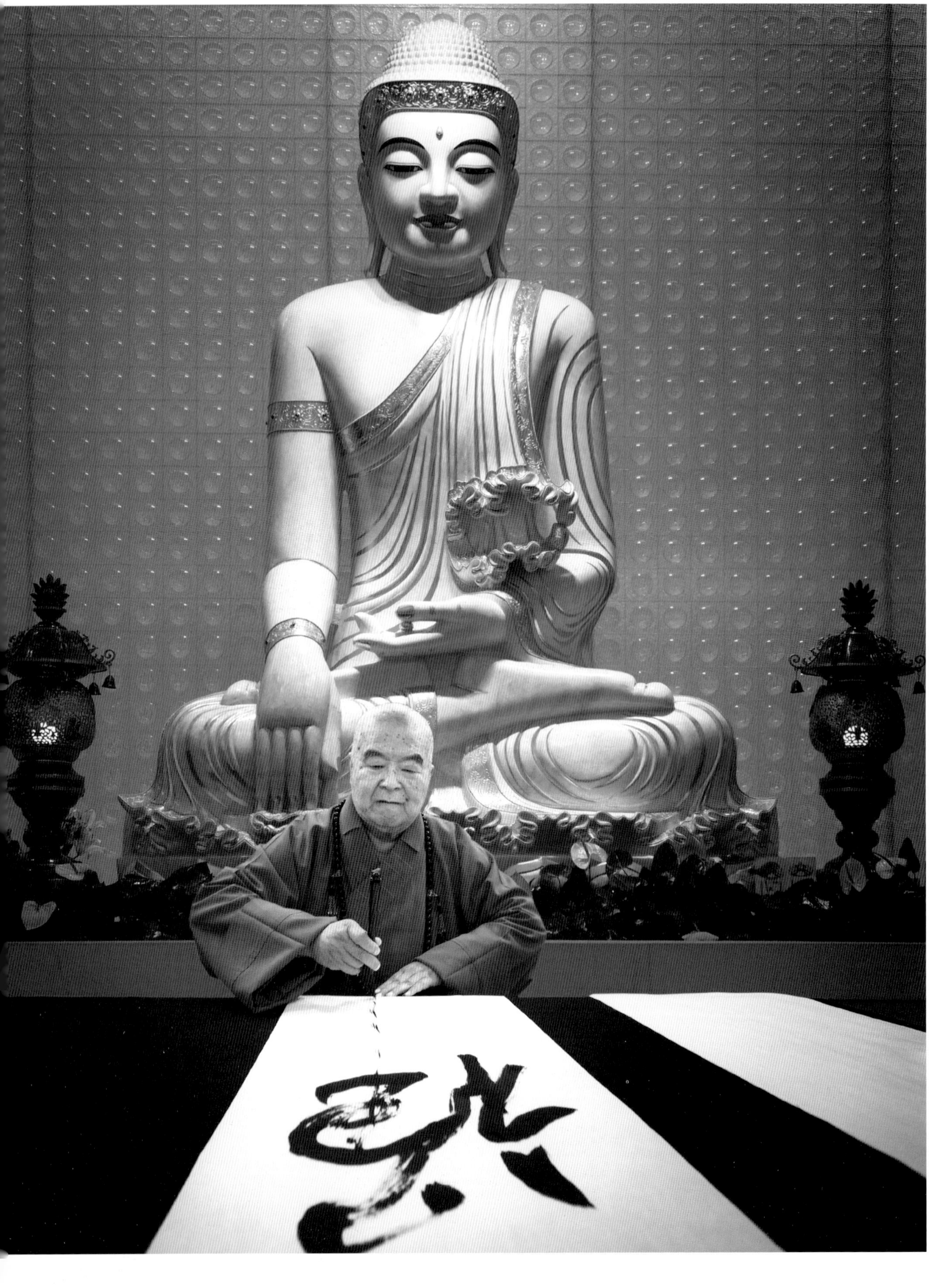

中國書法不但具有實用性，能供給人們在生活上的需要，並且與繪畫並列為中國藝術史的主流，自古以來是歷代皇室與庶民爭相蒐集的藝術品；它不僅能經過裝裱加框後，懸掛在廳堂、書齋之內供人欣賞，並且應用在各機關、商店等的招牌和名勝紀敘、碑誌等處，都有極高的藝術價值。

從善如流

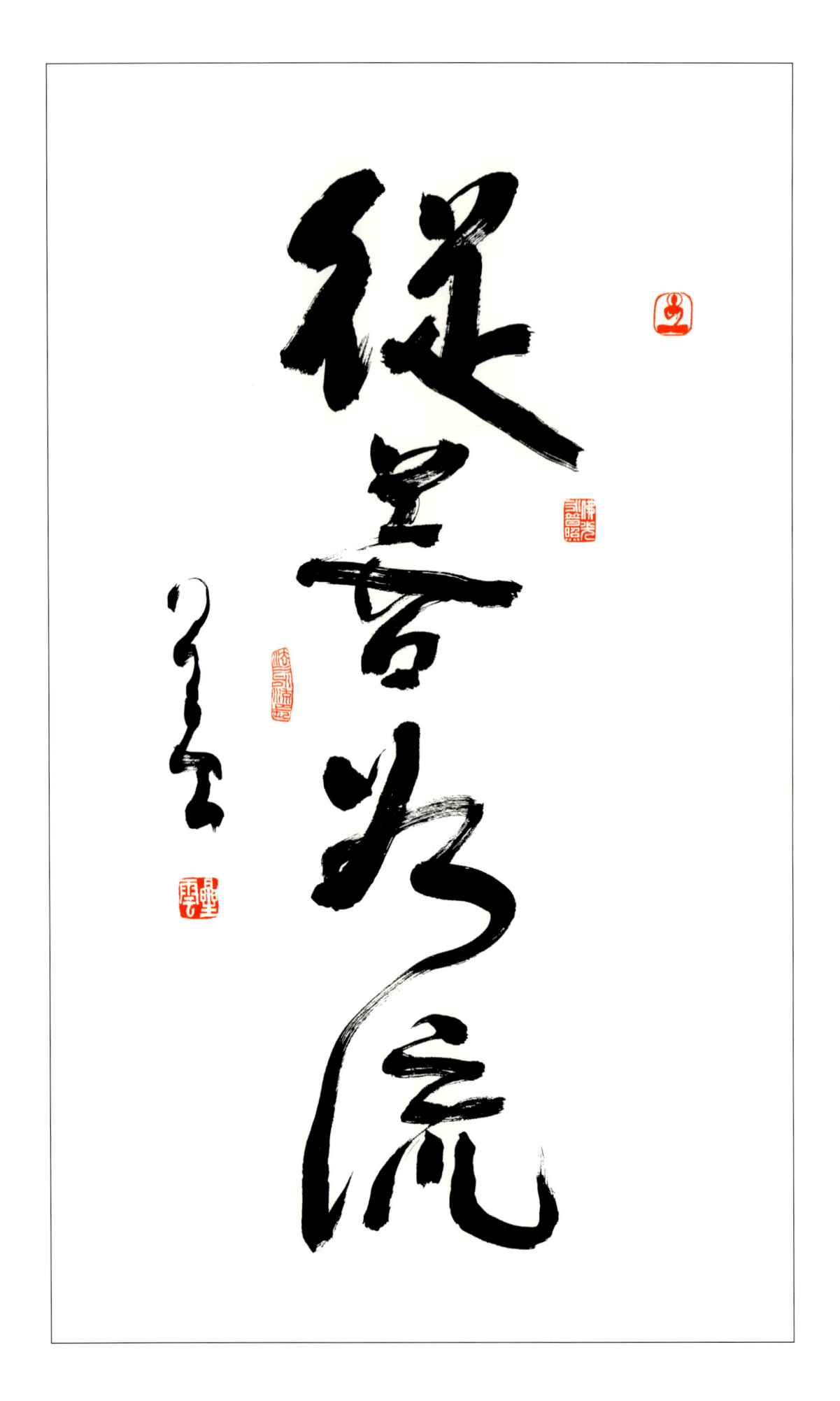

均鈐蓋「閒章」（佛光永普照、法水永流長），錯落有致，藉以烘托墨跡，使作品更可觀。（常用印：佛光永普照、法水永流長）

【白文印】

白文印又稱陰刻，就是將印章內的文字（線條）挖空，鈐蓋出白色的字，紅色的底，類似印刷所稱的凹板。（如：佛光永普照）

【朱文印】

朱文印又稱陽刻，就是將印章內的文字（線條）保留，其於部份（字底）刻去，類似印刷所稱的凸板。（如：法水永流長）

【創意】

傳統書法印章的鈐記，有其特定的位置，也就是前面所提到的「引首章」與「押角章」是指一般「閒章」。主要是與書法作品相互輝映；而大師為了豐富畫面，在書法作品每一行字之空間

【閑章】

除了姓名印之外，其餘的印章就稱為閑章，閑章實則不閑，好的閑章可收畫龍點睛之效，可與書法作品相互輝映，增加詩意，烘托神韻。閑章的內容很廣泛，有詩詞、佳句、成語、吉祥語，或者是圖像的，多以長方形、橢圓形或不規則等形式出現，有特定的鈐蓋位置。（如：阿彌陀佛造像）

【引首章及押角章】

印章，起源於夏商周三代及秦漢時期，有的吉祥語印式是屬於「閑章」，繁榮於清朝，通常鈐蓋於作品右上角，即作品第一方印者稱為「引首章」，有時右下角偶有出現閑章，則稱為押角章。
（如：佛陀造像、合掌菩薩）

伍・書法上的印章

書法作品除了墨跡（書者所寫的字）之外，有紅色的印記鈐蓋在不同的位置，有正方形、長方形、橢圓形，甚至有不規則形的，到底是什麼呢？答案就是印章鈐蓋，可區分兩種，一種是署款章，另一種是閑章。是中國書法藝術特徵之一，黑色字體搭配朱紅印章特別醒目，可增加美觀及充實作品畫面，可收相得益彰之效。

【署款章】

署款章也就是作者姓名印，作者完成書法作品後要簽署自己的名字，完成之後在署名的下方要鈐蓋一方印記，這方印就是署款章，通常是正方形的，代表端端正正之意。（如：星雲）

•「自在」，署款：星雲

【扇面】

此例為團扇，是最通行的手搖扇，面積不大，形狀大多是圓形，因為扇面所使用的材質是以細緻素絹製造而成，又稱為紈扇。傳統紈扇均以素絹製成，便於繪畫寫字。

【橫幅】

作品以橫向方式書寫，尺寸不一，視需要自定。

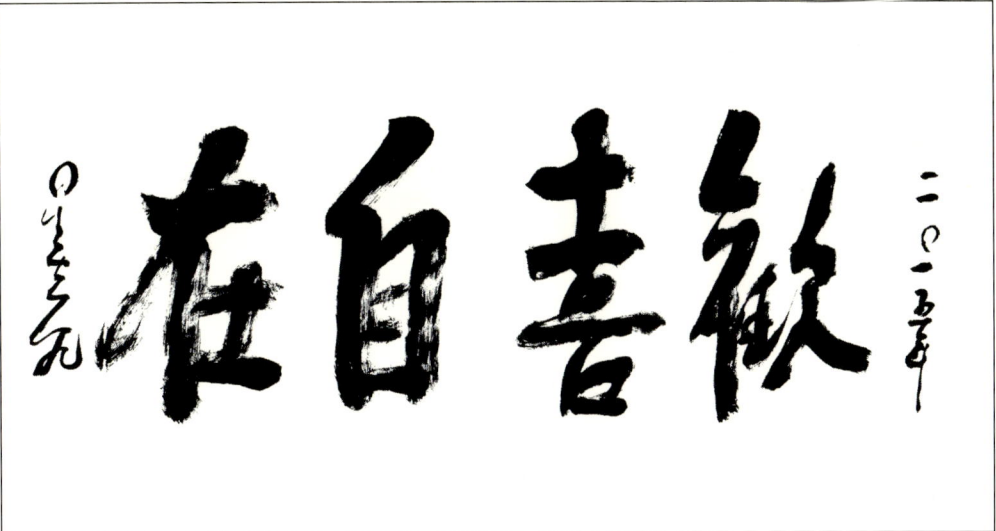

- 〈歡喜自在〉，雙款。
上款：二〇一五年；下款：星雲八九

【斗方】

格式方正者或接近正方形者均可稱斗方。

• 〈無我〉，署款：星雲

【條幅】

亦稱直幅或立幅，一般是長條形。

- 〈與人為善〉，署款：星雲八八

【對聯】

對聯也稱對句、對子等稱呼。是中國傳統文化之中具備生活化且有趣味的藝術表現形式,歷來受到人們的喜愛,適用範圍也很廣泛。中國民間每年除夕家家戶戶貼在大門兩側的春聯即是對聯,舊稱桃符,是為了趨吉避凶,宋朝王安石有詩云:「千門萬戶曈曈日,總把新桃換舊符。」就是形容此一民俗。

對聯的出現,本附會於時令民俗,園林景觀,或詩文繪畫等,經久歷時,逐漸成為一種獨立形式,備受文人雅士喜好,成為頗具特色的書法式樣。

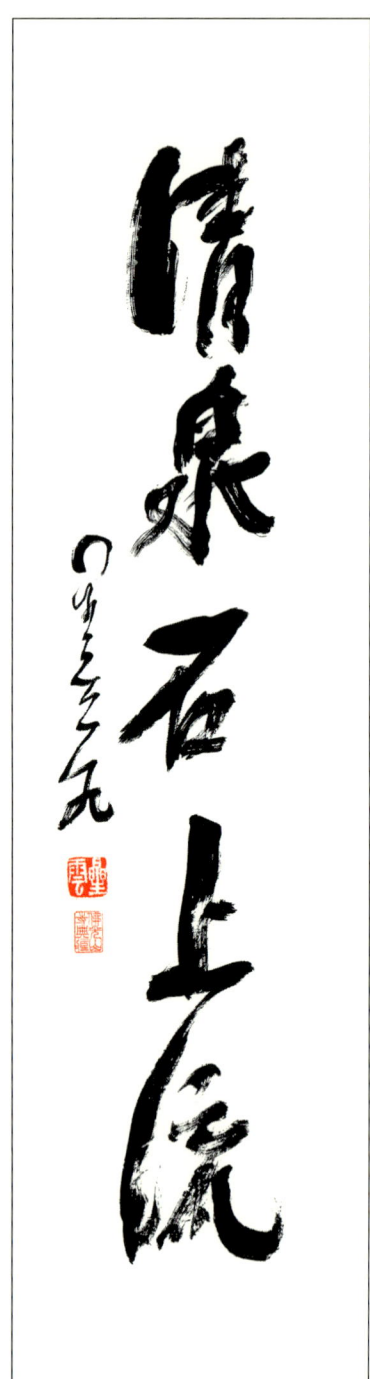

• 〈明月松間照,清泉石上流〉,署款:星雲八九

【何謂題款】

題款也稱「落款」，是整幅作品重要的有機組成部分，它不僅起著充實、穩正、烘托氣氛、陪襯主題的作用、甚至創作。

題款，一般分上款或下款，還有長款與短款。上款一般記述詩、詞名稱或被贈與者的名字；下款是記述書寫者姓名、年、月、作書地點等。若有下款而沒有上款稱「單款」，表示沒有特地贈送某人。

● 無盡藏，雙款。上款：南華圖書館；下款：星雲，一九九八

18

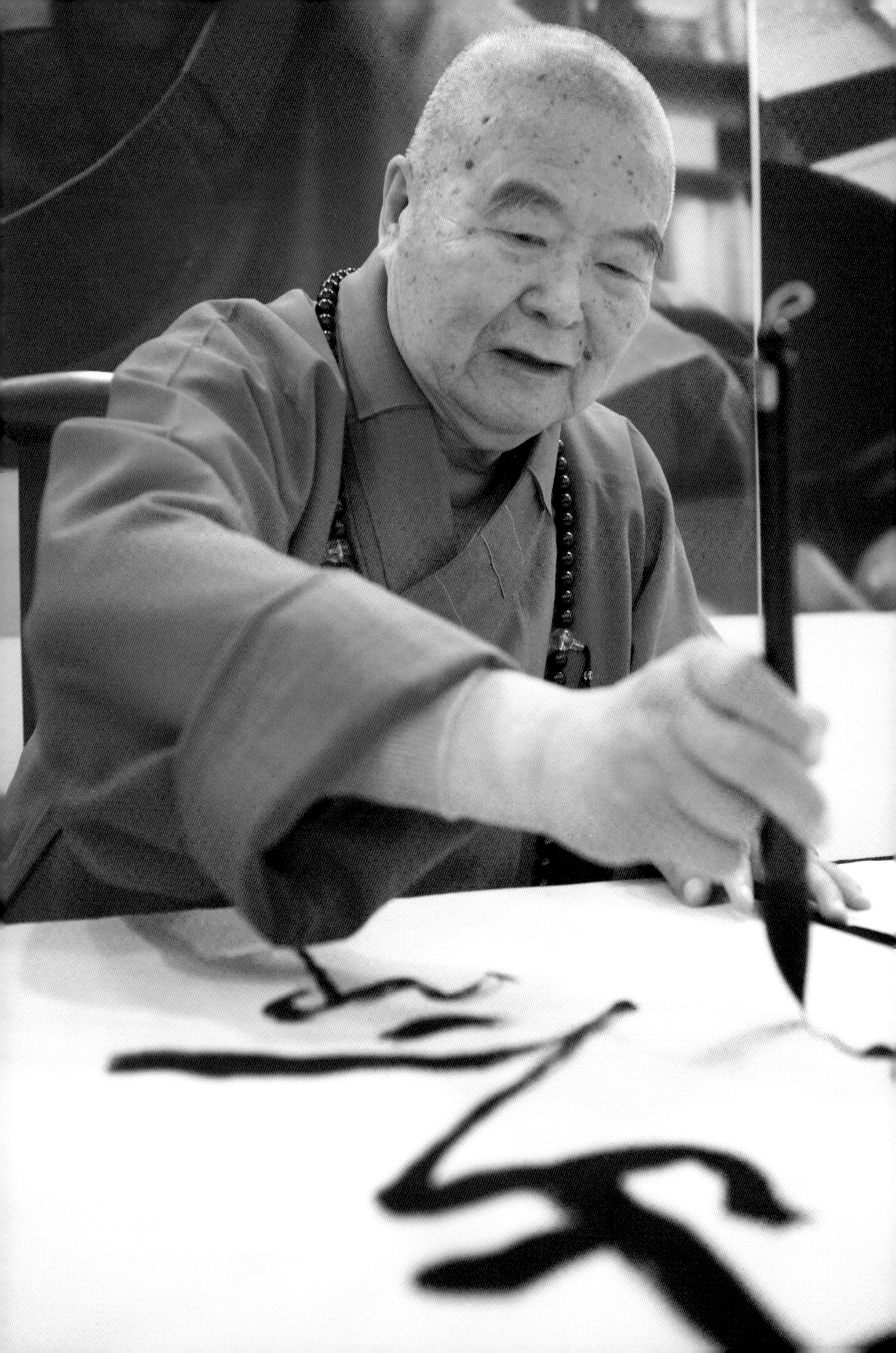

肆・中國書法的表現形式——生活化及有趣的藝術表現

書法從形象藝術的角度來看，它是繪畫，因為它能以豐富多姿的形象感動人心；就實用的角度來看，則它是文字。全世界只有獨特的中國字可當藝術品一般的欣賞，因為中國字每一個字就像是一幅畫。是我國特有的傳統藝術，不僅藝術的表現與西方不同，而所使用的材質也完全不同，運用可大可小的毛筆為工具書寫，將中國字特殊的結構，用墨將濃淡的線條組合在俱有渲染的白紙上。

一件書法作品不但在書藝上有不凡的造詣，同時也在文學上有相當的研究；這些不同內容的書法作品，通常是自撰的詩、詞、對聯、或者座右銘，引用名家的這類作品，而表現的形式也有不同名稱。

星雲大師扮演文化推手，透過充滿藝術的書法作品，每一幅字、每一句話如菩薩般慈悲的開示，將中國書法這東方文化特有的一項藝術瑰寶，由此推向世界的每一個角落。

【立軸格式】（裱褙材質有綾與緞）

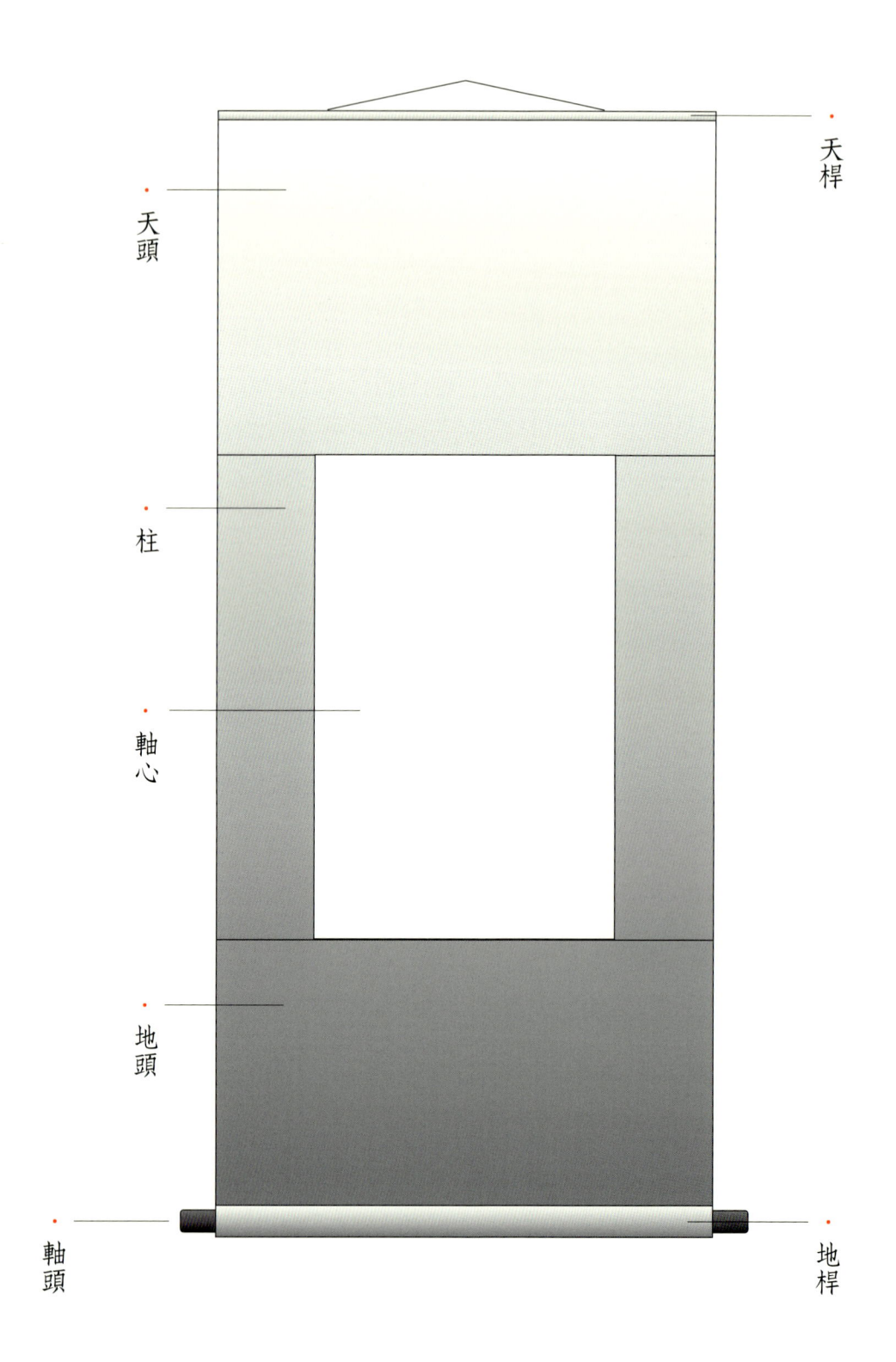

- 天桿
- 天頭
- 柱
- 軸心
- 地頭
- 軸頭
- 地桿

參·中國書畫的材質

傳統中國書畫所使用的材質有兩種，一種是「素絹」，另一種是「宣紙」；在紙未發明前，以絹作為書畫材質是非常普遍的，質細緻而優的絹是要送到宮中供皇室貴族使用，又稱為「宮絹」，一般人用的是黃絹。

【素絹】

【宣紙】

中國發明了紙始於東漢蔡倫，他的弟子孔丹繼承之後，在安徽涇縣以造紙為業，傳說有一次在山裡，偶見檀樹倒在溪邊，時間長久，都浸的發爛發白了，便想到以檀樹為造紙原料。經過不斷試驗改進，終於造出了上好的白紙，即後來的宣紙。

由於紙的普遍運用，使書法藝術也進入一個新發展階段，至唐朝開始大量生產，並正式稱為「宣紙」（安徽涇縣唐時稱宣州）。

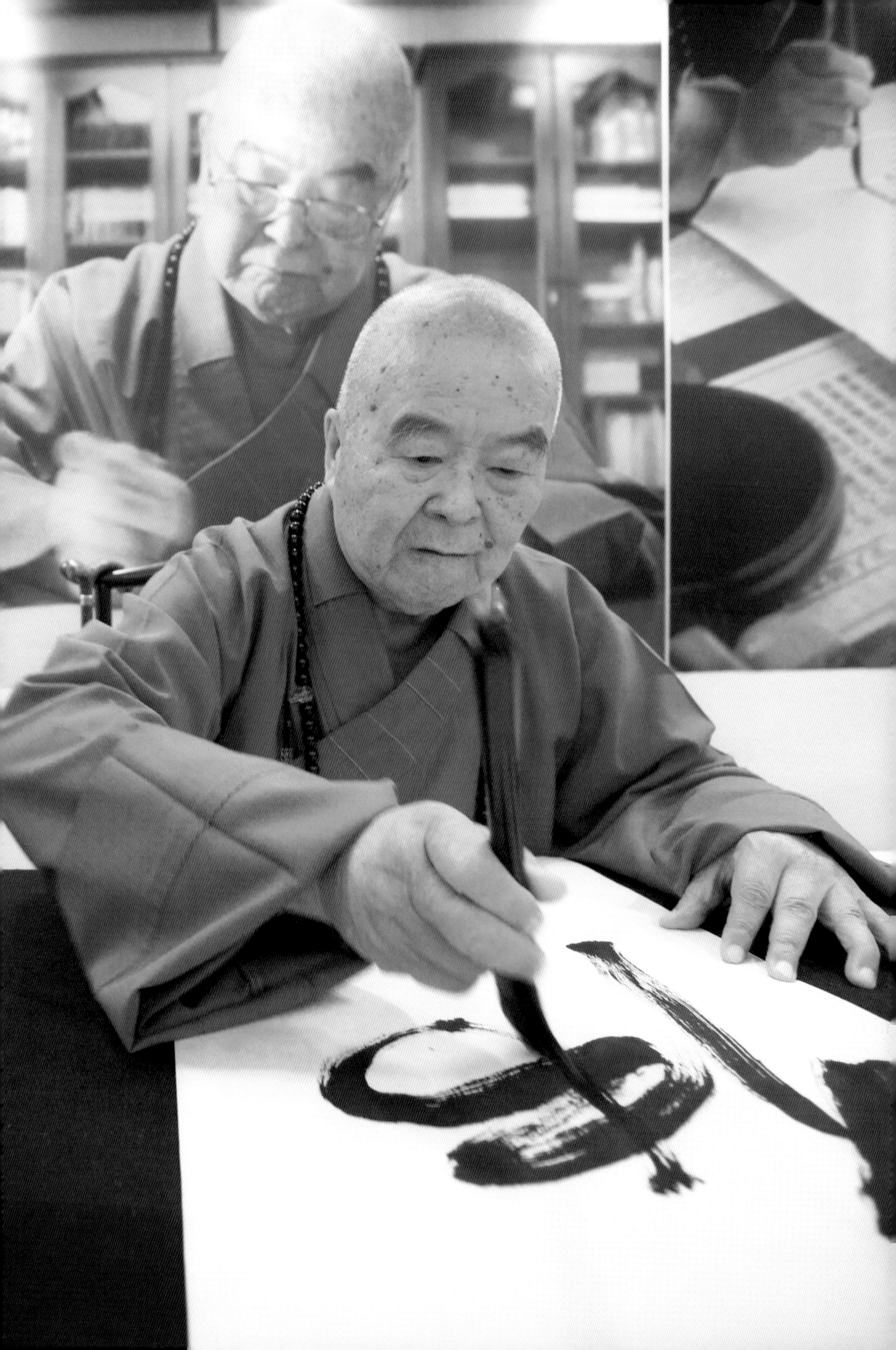

【星雲大師筆墨之感】

「有信眾從我的日記中,得知我常抽空寫字與人結緣,只要上山,就會帶幾枝毛筆、幾卷宣紙送我。因我不是行家,對此不懂考究,

筆,只要寫得順手;

紙,不要輕易滲透;

墨,有潤滑,就很滿足了。」

【筆】

筆很早就在中國出現。初時名稱也不統一，春秋戰國時楚地以「聿」名之。吳國稱「不律」、燕謂之「拂」。到了秦才稱為筆。戰國至秦漢，書官為求辦公方便，有把筆插在頭上的習慣。最初的毛筆，是在唐代以兔毫造筆。而羊毫則於宋代以後開始盛行。發展下來，不論鹿毛、狸、鼠、虎、狼、鵝、鴨、豬、雞、胎毛、髮、木、竹、茅等，都可以取毛用來造筆。使用新筆時必須注意兩點：一、因新筆有膠，可用涼水或溫水慢慢鬆開，切勿用開水去燙開，那樣會損傷鋒穎的彈性；二、每次寫完字應用清水將其洗刷乾淨，倒懸掛在筆架上。

【硯】

硯，又稱研，最早是研磨顏料的工具，後來發展成硯，材質有陶硯、石硯、瓦硯、磚硯、玉硯、瓷硯等，有方、圓、長方等。現在已經有墨汁，可注於硯台使用。使用時，必須以清水洗去硯面的浮灰，磨墨時圈子宜大，以防硯心處沉凹下去。清洗硯台宜用冷清水，不能用熱水，硯台切勿沾染油污，洗淨後不要用布、紙、棉擦磨，更不能曝曬。

石硯不用時，可在硯池中儲放清水及蓋上硯蓋，以保持濕潤。

貳・中國書畫的工具——文房四寶

【紙】

中國人發明指南針、火藥、造紙、印刷四大發明，其中兩項就和紙有關。中國還未有紙張時，都是用竹簡書寫。今天我們從右至左直行閱讀，就是保留當初在竹簡書寫，然後成冊的習慣。甚至書籍的頁面格式及行距都帶有竹簡痕跡。

【墨】

早在商周以前，墨作為一種供書寫的黑色顏料，中國畫用墨最重要。唐代製墨空前興盛，使墨發展出不少種類：有油煙墨、漆煙墨及松煙墨等。作畫最好用油煙墨。油煙墨用桐油煉煙和膠製成，黑而有光澤。漆煙墨的主要原料是漆，係墨中最黑者。松煙墨的主要原料是松木煙凝成的黑灰和膠做成，可用來寫書法。

墨要質地細、氣味清。放在陰乾之處，膠性可能保持長久一些。在畫扇面或絹上作畫，墨一定要新鮮。

● 星雲大師與一筆字墨跡

註：禁語

禁止自己說話。
禁語在於收攝口業，反觀自心，
故於禪堂參禪時，則須先禁語，
藉由禁語來約束身心，以達清淨自在。

• 星雲大師二十六歲書寫神情

【星雲大師書寫因緣】

星雲大師初到台灣，並住錫於宜蘭雷音寺，每年的佛七法會，殿堂裡、齋堂裡，有許多標語和對聯要寫。為了牆壁上貼「禁語」以及和念佛相關的法語，開始了寫毛筆字的因緣。

大師說：「我原本生性怯弱，不敢面對大眾，信徒請我寫標語齋條，我從未有練習書法的機會，但為了不讓他們失望，所以我先揣摩醞釀，然後小心下筆，不料一直寫到現在，徒眾們竟以擁有我的親筆墨跡為榮，弘法之暇，寫字送人成為我自娛娛人的興趣之一。後來更為了給人歡喜、祝願與感恩，寫字與眾結緣的墨跡不下千幅，更成為修行的一門功課。」

書法的演變

甲骨文 ——

金　文 ——

秦　篆 ——

隸　書 ——

楷　書 ——

行　書 ——

草　書 ——

甲骨文——指刻在龜甲和獸骨上的文字，是我國現存最古老的書體，其內容多與占卜有關。

金　文——指鑄造在青銅器上的文字。

秦　篆——是秦始皇統一中國後，通用全國的文字。字體結構整齊美觀，講究對稱。

隸　書——產生於戰國末年，是中國文字史上的重要變化。

楷　書——創於東漢末年，盛行於魏晉南北朝，隋唐最完備。楷是「楷模」、「標準」的意思。

行　書——行書介於楷書與草書之間，始於魏晉，經晉代王羲之父子發展而盛行。

草　書——西漢時期，人們為了方便快捷地書寫文字，將隸書結體變為簡約，筆畫出現牽帶鉤連的現象，但字與字之間相對獨立，並保留隸書的意味，這是中國草書的最初型態。

壹・前言——書法的由來

【書法的發展】

從古老的甲骨文時期到現代的網際網路,在華人世界裡所應用在平日生活的中國字,是沒有古今的分別,特殊的文字與書法藝術相互伴隨演進,它與中國文學及繪畫相互融會,在中國文化史上,有其長遠的重要地位,經過漫長歲月的累積已形成獨立系統。

夏商周三代是中國文字的成形時期,從占卜使用的甲骨文,到青銅器鑄造的鐘鼎文,各國有自己通行的文字,也就是金文;秦漢兩代是書法發展的關鍵時期,隨著秦始皇統一中國,結束金文的使用,在「書同文」的政策下,以小篆做為標準書體,中國字由此源頭開始發展。

春秋戰國時代新興書體——隸書逐漸產生,也在此一時期從小篆不斷簡化成熟,發展為漢代通行的書體,由於時代潮流趨向簡便快捷,隸書又蛻變分化,逐漸有楷書、行書、草書的形成。書體因應時代發展逐漸變化。因此進入魏晉南北朝之後,各體參雜的混合書法風格時而可見。

時序進入經貿發達民生富庶的隋唐時期,由於帝王對書法十分注重,此時的書法風貌南北各地書風匯集,朝向精緻形態發展,驅使楷書筆法相當完備,步入宋朝之後,文學高度發展,為了發揚前賢書風並得以長遠流傳,刻製碑帖日漸盛行。但是宋人並不以繼承傳統而滿足,書法取向表現個人性情、得其天趣。

元代繼起,轉而提倡復古,晉唐書法傳統受到重視,屬於反芻時期。至明代表現主義勢力擴張,使書法面貌至為紛雜,行草書尤其活躍,與傳統書風背離,其間突顯個性自成一格的書法家,也走出實現自己的道路,不為時代潮流所埋沒。

清代以降,三代及秦漢時期古文陸續出土,考古興盛,書法發展的視野得以串聯古今,當時書法家觀察古文字筆趣並嘗試新風格,終能在篆、隸書兩風格方面開創新方向。

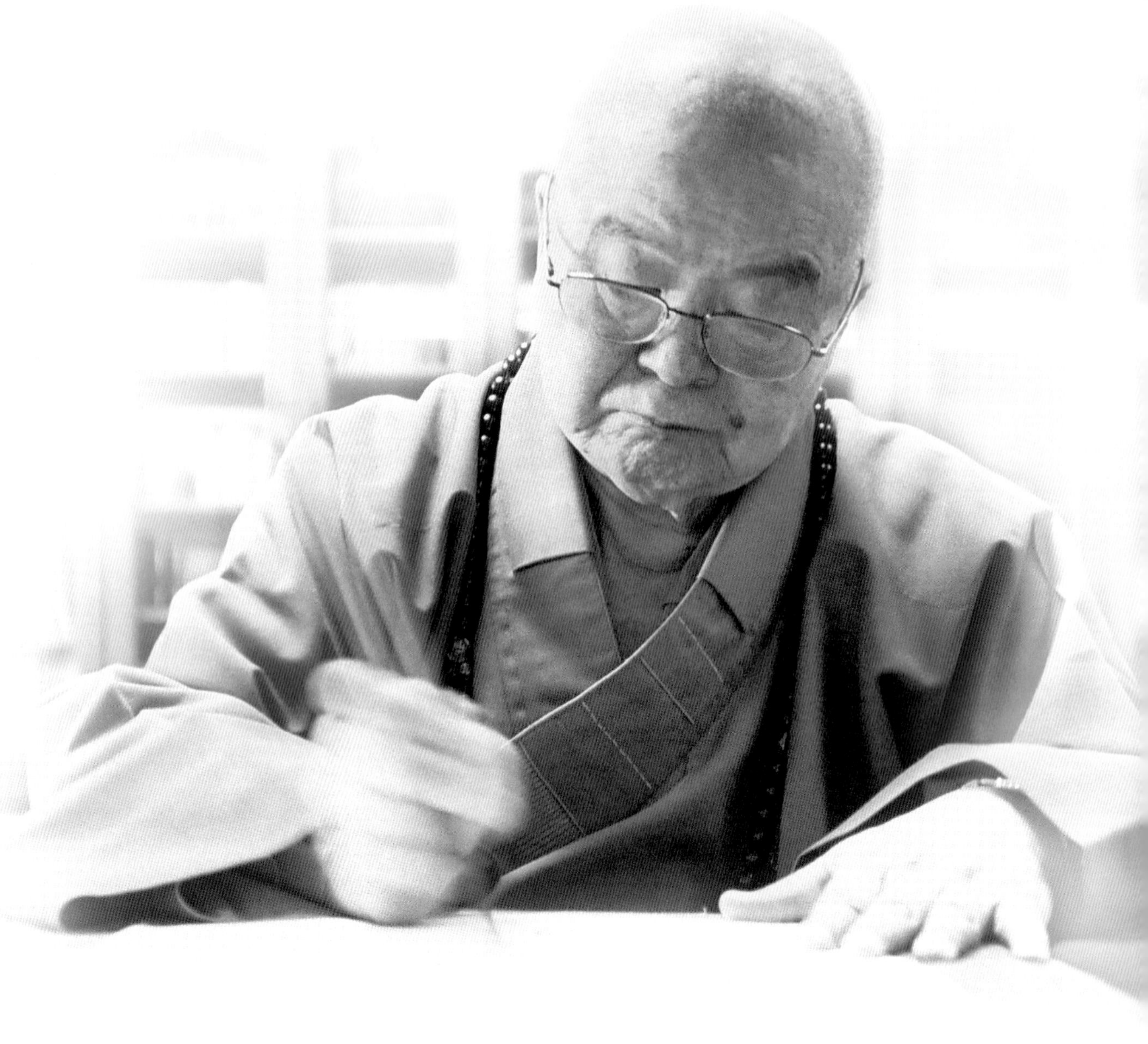

《非一般紙筆墨》編輯的話

「筆、墨、紙、硯文房四寶」為中國古代書寫工具，原以書寫為目的，最後卻形成中國特有的文化藝術——書法。

不同於一般寫字，書法從磨墨、醮墨到下筆，都具有收攝身心之功，因此也成為佛門修持的重要法門。早期佛教經典流佈所形成的寫經事業，更讓佛教與書法產生殊勝的因緣，及至現代許多寺院仍設有抄經堂，例如佛光山本山及各別分院也都設有抄經堂，備有筆墨紙硯供信眾抄經修持。

佛光山星雲大師一向重視中華傳統文化，大師自學書法從年輕至今未輟。然僧人寫書法並非始於今日，歷代祖師從懷素大師到近代弘一大師都是以書藝弘法的代表。因此星雲大師曾為文指出佛教對書法的兩大貢獻：一、保存書法文化；二、影響書法藝術創作。

由佛光緣美術館負責策畫辦理的「星雲大師一筆字書法展」十餘年來於全球各地舉辦，因為展出，「書法」這項傳統藝術再度吸引中外人士的關注，除欣賞外，從作品的書寫形式到篆刻章款也引起相關討論。因應大眾的需求，我們便著手規劃《非一般紙筆墨》的重新編纂再版，也將過去的口袋書形式，調整為較大的開本讓讀者易於收存。

星雲大師以書藝弘法，同時也將中國獨特的文字美學推廣到全世界，道藝一體，大化於無形。希望讀者在閱讀本書同時，不僅學習到書法的入門知識，也從大師的墨寶中薰習佛法大義。

國家圖書館出版品預行編目(CIP)資料

非一般紙筆墨：看星雲大師一筆字認識中國書法 / 釋如常主編. -- 再版. -- 高雄市：佛光山文教基金會出版：佛光緣美術館發行, 2020.05
　面；　公分
ISBN 978-957-457-549-7(平裝)

1.書法 2.佛教美術
224.52　　　　　　　　　　　109007003

非一般紙筆墨

書　　名	非一般紙筆墨
內頁書法	星雲大師
主　　編	如常
執行編輯	如川
文字編輯	陳俊光
英文翻譯	賴櫻丹、王玉梅、李貞慧、郎筱玲
英文校對	Annie Yang、張釗榮
美術設計	謝耀輝
書法攝影	薛湧
出　　版	財團法人佛光山文教基金會
發　　行	佛光緣美術館總部
地　　址	84049高雄市大樹區興田里興田路153號
電　　話	+886-7-656-1921分機1433
傳　　真	+886-7-656-5196
網　　站	http://fgsarts.fgs.org.tw
電子信箱	fgs_arts@ecp.fgs.org.tw
版　　次	二版2000本

出版日期：2020年7月
定　　價：新台幣490元

ISBN：978-957-457-549-7
版權所有　翻印必究

捌・〈星雲大師一筆字書法〉選輯　46

柒・星雲大師以書法為佛事　一筆字到病後字——認識星雲大師的美學思想　釋如常　星雲大師書法展歷　32

陸・以翰墨為佛事　傅申　30

伍・創意印章
創意　朱文印　白文印　引首章及押角章　閒章　署款章

書法上的印章　24

目次

壹．前言──書法的由來
　書法的發展
　書法的演變
　星雲大師書寫因緣
　　　　　　　　　　6

貳．中國書畫的工具──文房四寶
　紙、墨、筆、硯
　星雲大師筆墨之感
　　　　　　　　　　10

參．中國書畫的材質
　素絹
　宣紙
　立軸格式
　　　　　　　　　　14

肆．中國書法的表現形式──生活化及有趣的藝術表現
　何謂題款
　對聯
　條幅
　斗方
　橫幅
　扇面
　　　　　　　　　　16

非一般

紙筆墨

看星雲大師一筆字
認識中國書法